The Art of Dining in New Orleans

Joy Bateman

Author • Illustrator • Publisher

Whether therefore ye eat, or drink, or whatsoever ye do, do all to the glory of God.
I Corinthians 10:3

For Anna, Brown and William,
who keep me smiling with joy and pride
and
For Ben, who keeps me young

Also by Joy Bateman, The Art of Dining in Memphis

Copyright © 2007
Joy Bateman

Library of Congress Cataloging-in-Publication Data
ISBN 978-0-9773226-1-9

$21.95 plus S&H

Printed in the United States of America

Table of Contents

54 Mélange
Louisiana Crab Cake • Seafood Etouffée

56 Mulate's
Chicken and Sausage Jambalaya • Crawfish Etouffée • Fried Crawfish

58 The New Orleans Grill Room
Sea Scallops with Roasted Red Pepper Sauce

60 Pascal's Manale
Frutta Del Mare • Prosciutto Peppers and Shrimp

62 Peristyle
Chorizo Sausage Congris

64 The Restaurant at Victoria Inn
Seafood Gumbo • Lemon Meringue Pie

66 Restaurant Cuvée
Coq Au Vin Blanc • Mustard and Herb Crusted Salmon with Crab and Brie Orzo and Lemon Confit

68 Riche by Todd English
Frisée Aux Lardons

70 7 on Fulton
Chilled Creole Tomato Soup • Nine-Minute Cookies and Iced Milk

72 Stella!
Bananas Foster French Toast with Crispy Plantains and Spicy Candied Walnuts

74 Sully Mansion Bed and Breakfast
Creole Bread Pudding • French Toast

76 Tujague's
Crab and Spinach Bisque • Remoulade Sauce

78 Upperline
The Original Fried Green Tomato with Shrimp Remoulade • Syrup Cake (Gateau De Sirop)

Oysters Rockefeller was created at Antoine's. The dish was named after the richest baron of the day, John D. Rockefeller, as a comment on the richness of the sauce. Antoine's was founded in 1840 and is the oldest family owned restaurant in Nola. Despite the high altar tradition and hoop-la associated with Antoine's, owners and staff maintain an atmosphere of friendliness and warmth where guests feel most welcome and appreciated. The people at Antoine's are passionately upholding the Antoine's tradition of excellence. You can't go wrong at Antoine's. A glance at menu selections: Filet de truite meunière, Pompano grillé, Chateaubriand, Escargots à la Bourguignonne, Crabes mous grillés, Pommes de terre soufflés. Open for dinner Thursday, Friday, Saturday and Monday. Lunch on Fridays; Sunday Jazz Brunch.

Caramel Custard

Yield: 4 servings

Caramel Sauce:
6 ounces sugar
6 ounces water

In a small pot, cook sugar and water until caramelized (light brown). Distribute sauce evenly into 4 custard cups.

Custard:
4 eggs
6 ounces sugar
16 ounces half-and-half cream
1 teaspoon vanilla
Pinch of salt

Preheat oven to 340 degrees.

Heat cream (preferably in a double boiler) just until tiny bubbles form around the edge of pan. Be cautious to avoid boiling. Remove pan from heat immediately.

In a bowl, whip eggs, sugar, vanilla and salt.

Whipping constantly, slowly pour heated cream into egg mixture to incorporate.
Pour custard, dividing evenly, into the 4 custard cups with sauce.

Place the 4 cups of custard into a baking pan containing 1" or so of warm water.

Place pan in 340 degree oven and cook for 1 hour or until custard holds firm in center when shaken slightly. Chill cups of custard in refrigerator.

Garnish:
4 strawberries
Fresh mint leaves
Powdered sugar

To Serve:
Loosen custard edges with small knife. **Cooking Tip:** *To further ease removal, dip each cup quickly into hot water to depth of custard.* Turn each serving out onto a cold plate. Garnish each with mint leaves, a strawberry and a sprinkling of powdered sugar.

Pompano Pontchartrain

Yield: 4 servings

4 8-ounce pompano fillets
Oil
Salt
White pepper

Sprinkle oil, salt and pepper on fillets.
Cook on hot grill or flat skillet for 3-4 minutes on each side, or until done.

Crabmeat Topping:
12 ounces jumbo lump crabmeat
6 ounces melted butter
2 ounces chopped green onions
Juice of 1 lemon
Salt and pepper to taste

Cook green onions in butter for 1-2 minutes. Add crabmeat, lemon juice, salt and pepper. Remove pan from heat as soon as crabmeat heats through. Be cautious not to overheat.

For Garnish:
1 lemon, quartered
Parsley

To Serve:
Place each pompano fillet on a plate; ladle Crabmeat Topping onto each fillet.
Garnish each serving with parsley and lemon wedge.

Antoine's Restaurant

713 Rue Saint Louis • New Orleans 70130 • Tel 504-581-4422

Creole cuisine at its finest. Warm, crisp French bread, gift-wrapped in white linen napkins, sets the stage for dinner at Arnaud's. Consider the signature dish, Shrimp Arnaud, with its original Creole remoulade called simply, "Arnaud's Sauce." Fortunately, Arnaud's has bottled this stuff, so you can take some home, if you like (or see www.arnauds.com to order). There's more on the menu, though. Keep reading and you'll find Alligator Sausage, in-house creation Oysters Ohan, Creole Crabcakes, Crawfish O'Connor, Gulf Snapper Pontchartrain, Pompano en Croute, Rock Cornish Game Hen Whitecloud, Veal Tournedos Chantal, Soufflé Potatoes, Smothered Okra, Creamed Spinach and much more. Arnaud's shines with Southern tradition: exuberant, first class Creole food served in dining rooms graced with romantic antique chandeliers and ceiling fans. Open for lunch and dinner.

Petit Filet Mignon Lafitte

Yield: 6 servings

6 filets mignons, about 5 ounces each
¼ cup clarified butter
Salt and black pepper
3 dozen oysters, drained
1 cup flour seasoned with 1 teaspoon salt and ½
   teaspoon white pepper
Vegetable oil for frying oysters
1 ½ cups Creole Sauce Robert (recipe follows)

Heat 6 dinner plates in warm oven. Season filets on
both sides with salt and pepper. Heat butter in sauté
pan over high heat. Cook filets to order: rare, 3-5
minutes per side; medium rare, 5-6 minutes per side;
medium, 7-8 minutes per side; medium well, 7-9
minutes per side; well done, 9-11 minutes per side.
While filets are cooking, dredge oysters in seasoned
flour and shake off excess. In a skillet filled to 2"
depth with vegetable oil heated to 350 degrees, fry
oysters until golden brown (about 3-4 minutes). Keep
warm.

To Plate:
Transfer a filet to a hot dinner plate and slice in half
horizontally. Place 2 fried oysters between halves of
filet and arrange 4 more oysters on plate around filet.
Ladle about ¼ cup Creole Sauce Robert over filet;
serve immediately.

Creole Sauce Robert

Yield: 1 quart

Note: *Creole Sauce Robert is essential to many Creole
recipes. To keep on hand, make 1 quart of sauce and
store frozen in 1 cup quantities.*

1/8 cup olive oil
1 cup chopped white onion
½ cup diced green peppers
1 ½ cups chopped celery
½ cup chopped fresh parsley
1 clove garlic, chopped
2 cups veal stock
¾ teaspoon chicken base or granulated chicken
   bouillon
1 bouquet garni, consisting of ½ bunch parsley, 3 bay
   leaves, 1 sprig fresh thyme and 1 stalk celery
½ cup diced tomatoes
1 ½ cups tomato purée
Salt and freshly ground black pepper, cayenne and
   Tabasco to taste

Heat olive oil in 2-quart saucepan over high heat. Add
onions, green pepper, celery and parsley. Cook and stir
for 2 minutes; add garlic. Add veal stock, chicken base
or bouillon, bouquet garni, diced tomatoes and tomato
purée and bring to boil. Reduce heat and simmer
10 minutes. Add salt, freshly ground black pepper,
cayenne and Tabasco to taste.

Arnaud's

813 Rue Bienville • New Orleans 70112 • Tel 504-523-0377

Renowned Chef Susan Spicer, sassy and saucy as ever, keeps on keeping on with her high standards of excellence. A recipient of both the Golden Whisk Award and the Ivy Award, Chef Spicer was named Best Chef: Southeast (1993) by the James Beard Foundation. Bayona has just been listed in *1,000 Places to See in the U.S.A. and Canada Before You Die* (Workman Publishing, May 2007). At Bayona, everything is so consistently good, I never know what to order. Usually, I just go with the specials. However, the Sautéed Pacific Salmon with Choucroute and Gewurztraminer Sauce, Chef Spicer's signature dish, definitely comes to mind when I think of Bayona. Well worth attention are Chef Spicer's glorious soups. I offer more than mere praise for these---I crown her Queen of Soups!

Crispy Smoked Quail Salad

Yield: 4 servings

Marinated and Smoked Quail:
1 tablespoon honey
1 tablespoon sweet soy (Indonesian Ketjap Manis)
¼ cup peanut oil
1 tablespoon Bourbon
4 quail, partially boned

Whisk together all marinade ingredients in a small bowl.
Turn the quail in the marinade. Let rest at least 1 hour.
Drain the quail and cold smoke for about ½ hour. The quail should still be mostly raw.

Bourbon Molasses Dressing:
1 pound quail or chicken bones
1 cup chicken stock
2 tablespoons molasses
2 tablespoons cider vinegar
1 tablespoon walnut vinegar
  (if not available, add
1 more tablespoon cider vinegar)
1 tablespoon finely chopped shallots
2/3 cup olive oil
1 tablespoon Bourbon

Brown bones in the oven; then place them in a small pot and cover with chicken stock and 1 cup water. Bring to a boil, then lower heat and simmer, reducing the liquid in the pot to about 3 tablespoons. Separate this syrupy liquid from the bones by straining it into a bowl. (Discard the bones.) Whisk molasses, vinegars, shallots and oil into the bowl with the reduced liquid. Season to taste with salt and pepper. Stir in Bourbon.

Spiced Pecans for Garnish:
½ cup pecans
2 teaspoons butter
1 teaspoon L&P Worcestershire Sauce
½ teaspoon salt
2 tablespoons sugar
¼ teaspoon cayenne pepper

Melt butter and toss with pecans and all other ingredients. Spread out on a small baking sheet and roast in a 350 degree oven for 10 minutes or so, until lightly toasted.

Rice Flour Batter:
½ cup rice flour
½ cup water
¼ teaspoon salt
Pinch of pepper

Whisk tempura batter ingredients together.

Fried Quail:
Pat Marinated and Smoked Quail dry on paper towels.
Dip each quail in Rice Flour Batter and fry in 350 degree oil for 3-4 minutes.
Drain quail on paper towels. Cut each quail into quarters.

Completed Salad:
4 cups mixed greens, washed and dried
¼ cup pickled red onion
½ cup celery hearts and leaves, chopped
Bourbon Molasses Dressing
1 ripe pear, cored and cut into 16 thin wedges
Fried Quail
Spiced Pecans

Toss salad greens with red onion, celery and some of the Bourbon Molasses Dressing.
Arrange 4 pear wedges on each of 4 salad plates.
Divide salad greens among plates and place one Fried Quail on each salad.
Drizzle salads with a little more dressing and sprinkle with Spiced Pecans.

Bayona

430 Dauphine St. • New Orleans, 70112 • Tel 504-525-4455

After a serving of Begue's Artichoke Velouté, all I wanted was more Artichoke Velouté. No surprise, this Artichoke Velouté won "Best in Show" at the 2006 New Orleans Wine and Food Experience Grand Tasting. In a righteous display of self-discipline, I studied the entrées. Begue's Framboise Roasted Bison, Rib Eye and House Smoked Salmon and English Cucumber Roulade are all very tasty. An amuse-bouche that Chef Joseph Maynard brought to my table tempted me to sing a little song in its praises. I planned to return soon for the Pan Roasted Filet Mignon "atop a terrine of duck liver, pork, dried cherries and orange with crispy Grape leaf, peeled white grape, balsamic tomato reduction." Begue's, located in the middle of The Royal Sonesta in New Orleans, is one of only a handful of in-hotel restaurants that is even mentioned in *Zagat 2007/2008 World's Top Hotels, Resorts and Spas*. Luxurious yet welcoming atmosphere, with piano music.

Pan Roasted Veal Rib Eye with Chive & Garlic Oil Smashed Yukon Potatoes, Parsnip Purée & Apple Bacon Bordelaise Sauce

Yield: 4-6 servings

Veal Rib Eye:
4-6 6-ounce veal rib eye steaks
1 ounce olive oil
1 tablespoon unsalted butter
Kosher salt to taste
Black pepper to taste

Method:
Preheat oven to 350 degrees.
Rub steaks with olive oil and season to taste with salt and pepper. Melt butter over high heat in large ovenproof skillet. Sear steaks on both sides.
Place skillet in 350 degree oven and allow to steaks to continue to cook until they reach desired temperature.

Chive and Garlic Oil Potatoes:
6 Yukon Gold potatoes
1 ounce chives, minced
2 ounces garlic-infused olive oil
1 cup heavy cream
1 pound unsalted butter
Kosher salt to taste
Black pepper to taste

Method:
Boil potatoes until tender enough to mash.
Pass potatoes through a ricer. Heat butter and heavy cream just to boiling point (bubbles will begin to form around edge of pan); do not allow to boil. Add chives and garlic-infused olive oil. Blend riced potatoes with cream mixture. Season to taste with salt and pepper. Keep warm until ready to serve.

Parsnip Purée:
4 parsnips
1 shallot, minced
2 cloves garlic, minced
½ cup heavy cream
¼ cup Mascarpone cheese

Method:
Peel and dice parsnips. Place all ingredients except Mascarpone cheese in a small pot. Cook until tender; set aside to cool.
Once cool, place mixture in blender and purée on high until smooth. Add Mascarpone and blend thoroughly.

Apple Bacon Sauce:
2 ounces carrots
2 ounces celery
4 ounces onion
8 ounces apple smoked bacon
½ ounce shallots, minced
12 ounces red wine
1 quart demiglace
Salt to taste
Pepper to taste
Sugar to taste
Rice wine vinegar to taste

Method:
Brown bacon in saucepan over medium heat until crisp. Remove from pan. Add aromatic vegetables and sweat them until they are lightly caramelized. Deglaze pan with red wine and vinegar. Season sauce with salt, pepper and sugar; reduce liquid by ¾. Add demiglace and reduce by ½ over medium heat. Add sugar to counteract any bitterness. Strain through a fine mesh sieve and serve.

Flowering Plant at Royal
Sonesta Hotel, New Orleans

Begue's

300 Bourbon St. • New Orleans 70130 • Tel 504-586-0300

At the heart of The Bistro at Maison de Ville is New Orleans native, Chef Greg Picolo. Inordinately passionate, talented and kind, Chef Picolo offers a menu of haute Louisiana Creole dishes. The restaurant and the kitchen are small. The Bistro is a proper venue for a romantic, intimate occasion or for a small business dinner where superb food is *sine qua non*. Chef Picolo's creative menu deserves the massive applause it regularly receives. Until I manage to try everything on the menu, I will feel that I am missing out. The Avocado, Grilled Grapefruit, Cucumber and Lump Crabmeat Salad served with a Classic French Vinaigrette is an uplifting experience. Among the entrées, notice the Grilled Scallops in a Fennel, Italian Sausage, Roasted Corn and Saffron Butter Broth served with Sautéed Arugula and Truffle Scented Risotto Alfredo. How about a little dessert? On the menu: Cappuccino Cream Cheese Brownie with Patron Tequila Mocha Soup. The Bistro is a jewel in the crown of the French Quarter, perhaps the best kept secret of post-Katrina New Orleans dining.

Moules Frites, or Mussels and French Fries

Yield: 4-6 servings

8-12 pounds fresh mussels
2-4 tablespoons minced fresh garlic
1-3 tablespoons minced fresh Italian flat leaf parsley
2-4 cups dry white wine
½-1 pound unsalted butter
Salt and pepper to taste
5 large potatoes
Peanut oil, for deep frying
Mayonnaise

Chef's Comment: *This is a dish that combines Italian style of mussels with a nod to Belgium, with the addition of French fries and mayonnaise as garnish.*

Peel potatoes and cut into batonnets. Reserve potatoes in a large bowl of cold water, to prevent oxidation prior to frying.

Clean mussels in very cold ice water. Cleaning and sorting mussels meticulously is the most critical step in preparing this dish. Any mussel with an open shell is inedible: discard all such mussels. Scrub remaining mussels and remove all traces of beards. Reserve cleaned mussels in refrigerator.

To fry potatoes, heat peanut oil to 375 degrees.

Dry potatoes with paper towels and fry them until cooked and golden brown, about 12-16 minutes. Depending on the size of pan, you may need to fry potatoes in batches.

While French Fries are cooking, combine wine, garlic and parsley in a large covered pot, such as a lobster steamer. Simmer mixture 2-3 minutes, to allow flavors to develop. Add salt, pepper and butter to mixture; add mussels. Steam, covered, for 3-6 minutes. Shells should be barely open. Remove pot from heat.

To Serve:
Divide steamed mussels evenly among 4-6 large individual serving bowls. Top each serving with French Fries and garnish with mayonnaise. Serve immediately.

The Bistro at Maison de Ville

727 Rue Toulouse • New Orleans 70130 • Tel 504-528-9206

15

Bon Ton Café

The Bon Ton is an old friend. Make new friends, but… I have fond memories of visits with child in tow, dating back to the late '70's. Business people meet there to wheel and deal over lunch, Mondays through Fridays. Business suits rule, but the dress code is casual. A memorable and happy accident befell me here years ago: I intended to order fried shrimp, but somehow I ended up with a plate of oysters. I was sure I didn't like oysters, until I bit into those. Best damn fried oysters this side of heaven. For foodies out for great Crawfish Etouffée, the Bon Ton is a surefire destination. Then there's the very popular Bread Pudding with Whiskey Sauce. To die for. Don't get me started. Owners Debbie and Wayne Pierce are the perfects hosts.

Homemade Turtle Soup

Yield: 8-10 bowls

Chef's Note: *Quantities may be doubled and soup frozen for future use.*

1.5 gallons water

2 cups tomato sauce

2 cups whole peeled tomatoes, chopped

2 ½ cups dried onions

5 bay leaves

2 ½ pounds turtle meat (or beef, such as brisket), cut into small pieces, almost diced

¼ cup cloves, wrapped in tightly sealed cloth

½ dozen hard boiled eggs, diced

1 lemon, cut into 5-7 slices

1 cup chopped parsley

Salt and pepper to taste

1 cup sherry cooking wine

3 cups roux (made with 2 cups flour and 2 cups vegetable oil)

Bring one gallon of water to boil in large pot. Add tomato sauce, chopped tomatoes, dried onions and bay leaves. Bring to simmer.

Roux:

Combine flour and oil in a skillet.

Heat over low to medium flame, stirring often to prevent burning.

You may have to add oil to keep consistency of roux slightly loose.

When roux is golden brown, remove from heat.

Add roux to simmering mixture and stir to combine thoroughly. Add turtle meat and simmer for 1 hour. Add eggs, lemon slices, sealed pouch of cloves, salt and pepper. Simmer ½ hour longer, stirring frequently to keep roux well dissolved and other ingredients evenly distributed throughout soup.

Turn off heat.

Remove lemon slices and pouch of cloves. Add parsley and cooking sherry. Adjust seasoning to taste.

Cooking Options:

For a thinner soup, dilute with water to achieve preferred consistency.

For more intense flavor and/or thicker soup, cook a bit longer to allow further reduction.

Bon Ton Café

401 Magazine St. • New Orleans 70130 • Tel 504-524-3386

When in Rome, do as the Romans do. When in New Orleans, have breakfast at Brennan's. Memories of this special meal will stay with you for a long time. Choose from among the lavish egg dishes: Eggs Sardou, Eggs Hussarde, Eggs St. Charles, Eggs Benedict, Cajun Andouille Crabmeat Omelette, Cajun Tasso Omelette with Cheddar Cheese. The menu offers far more than tantalizing egg entrées, though. Look for Grillades and Grits, Brennan's Blackened Redfish, Oysters Benedict and Trout Nancy — "fresh sautéed trout topped with lump crabmeat sprinkled with capers, lemon butter sauce." Consider a variety of succulent soups and gumbos, as well, and save room for one of the flaming desserts, such as Brennan's own famed Bananas Foster. Open for breakfast, lunch and dinner. Note: Brennan's is closed Tuesdays and Wednesdays in the summer.

Baked Macaroni Annie

Yield: 8-10 servings

2 quarts water
1 pound #1 elbow macaroni
12 eggs
2 cups heavy cream (or Pet® milk)
Salt and white pepper
1 pound sharp cheddar cheese, cubed
½ cup (1 stick) butter
Optional: extra sliced cheddar for top of casserole

Preheat oven to 400 degrees.
Bring 2 quarts water to boil. Add macaroni and cook, stirring frequently, 7-10 minutes, until tender. Drain macaroni in colander.
In large mixing bowl, beat eggs slightly, then add cream. Season mixture with salt and pepper to taste. Stir in cheese, then add macaroni and toss.
Slice butter and place pats in bottom of a 13" x 9" x 2" baking dish. Pour macaroni mixture into dish. Optionally, top with slices of cheese. Place baking dish in a larger pan containing ½" of water. Bake mixture until set and slightly browned, 35-45 minutes.

Bananas Foster

Yield: 4 servings

¼ cup (1/2 stick) butter
1 cup brown sugar
½ teaspoon cinnamon
¼ cup banana liqueur
4 bananas, cut in half lengthwise, then halved
¼ cup white rum
4 scoops vanilla ice cream

In a flambé pan or skillet, combine butter, sugar and cinnamon. Place pan over low heat either on an alcohol burner or on top of stove.

Cook, stirring, until sugar dissolves. Stir in banana liqueur, then place bananas in pan. While bananas are cooking, place 1 scoop of ice cream in each of 4 individual serving dishes and set aside.
When banana sections soften and begin to brown, carefully add rum. Continue to cook sauce until rum is hot. Tilt pan away from yourself and ignite rum. When flames subside, lift bananas from pan and place 4 pieces of banana over each portion of ice cream. Generously spoon warm sauce over servings of ice cream and serve immediately.

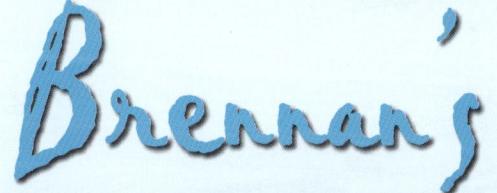

417 Royal St. • New Orleans 70130 • Tel 504-525-9711

Broussard's first opened in 1920. I go back a long way with Broussard's, to my wedding night dinner there in October, 29 years ago. Current proprietors Gunter and Evelyn Preuss proudly uphold Broussard's long-standing tradition of offering the finest in classic French and Provençal cuisine. They have added sassy touches to the menu, incorporating innovative dishes without abandoning the classics. Some current menu items: Trio of New Orleans Oysters: Three Fried Oysters served Rockefeller, Bienville and Broussard's Style; Cappucino Style Corn, Shrimp and Sweet Potato Bisque; Pompano Broussard's; Crabmeat Ravigote; Creole Mustard Braised Porkchop. For a special holiday celebration, reserve your table for Broussard's German Christmas Réveillon Menu of traditional German style entrées, with traditional Christmas decorations in the "Courtyard of Lights." (The Réveillon Menu begins early in December; call Broussard's for details.)

Bouillabaisse

Yield: 6 servings

Broth:
½ pound carrots
½ pound celery ribs
½ pound fennel
½ pound onions
½ pound green peppers
½ cup olive oil
1 tablespoon chopped garlic
¼ cup chopped shallots
½ cup tomato paste
1 gallon lukewarm shrimp or fish stock
2 cups chopped tomatoes
1/8 ounce saffron
Salt and white pepper to taste
3 bay leaves

Steep saffron in hot water.
Peel and split carrots, then slice them diagonally.
Slice celery ribs diagonally.
Cut onions, fennel and green peppers into thin slices.
In a large stock pot, heat olive oil and sauté carrots,
celery and fennel until halfway cooked.
Add onions, peppers, garlic and shallots.
When mixture is thoroughly heated, stir in tomato
paste and cook for 10 minutes, stirring regularly.
Add lukewarm stock.
Add tomatoes, crushing and draining by hand as you go.
Add saffron (already steeped), salt, pepper and bay leaves.
Bring to full boil.
Remove from heat.
Cool and chill.

Seafood for Bouillabaisse:
1 pound peeled, deveined raw shrimp
1 cup raw oysters
½ pound lump crabmeat
½ pound peeled crawfish tail meat
½ pound fresh fish (trout, pompano, etc.),
  cut into 1" cubes
½ pound raw scallops
18 fresh mussels

To Complete Bouillabaisse:
In a soup pot, heat the broth to a boil.
Add all seafood.
Now bring the mixture to a simmer
and cook for approximately 5 minutes,
long enough for the seafood to be
cooked but not overdone.

Serve and enjoy!

Broussard's

819 Conti St. • New Orleans 70112 • Tel 504-581-3866

Located inside the historic Hotel Monteleone, Le Café outdoes all contenders for "best breakfast buffet," in my humble opinion. Just when you think you have tasted the most delectable treat on the buffet, you find something that's even better. Am I smiling, or what? Boudin (BOO-dan) is a rich and well seasoned rice and pork sausage for which we must thank all Cajuns. Some divine Boudin, perfectly grilled tomatoes, a massive, marvelous assortment of fresh fruits, particularly flavorful asparagus, assorted baked pastries and grits with country gravy, all make for an unforgettable breakfast. Follow up with a luscious lunch at Le Café and then move on to Hotel Monteleone's Carousel Piano Bar and Lounge, where you can ride the brightly colored merry-go-round while sipping a mint julep and listening to piano music. Back in the 1940's, the Carousel Lounge became a top attraction as New Orleans' first revolving bar, worthy of its mention in *1,000 Places in the U.S.A. and Canada to See Before you Die* (Workman Publishing, May 2007).

Seafood and Fried Okra Gumbo

Yield: 12 servings

Ingredients, by Category:

For Gumbo Base--
3 ½ quarts fish stock
2 cups Dark Brown Roux (recipe follows)
2 ounces chopped garlic
5 bay leaves
5 sprigs thyme
½ cup filé powder, dissolved in water

For Dark Brown Roux--
1 cup flour
1 cup margarine

For Garnish--
1 large onion, diced
½ bunch celery, diced
2 Creole tomatoes, seeded and diced
2 green peppers, sliced
2 ounces salad oil

Seafood--
¾ pound crawfish tails
1 pound medium shrimp
¾ pound backfin crabmeat

Fried Okra--
2 cups okra, chopped

1 cup flour, seasoned with salt and pepper
3 eggs
1 cup water
2 cups Cajun corn flour

Final Seasoning--
Cayenne, salt and pepper to taste

Method of Preparation:

Brown Roux:
Melt margarine in baking pan and mix in flour evenly. Bake in oven at 400 degrees for 45 minutes, stirring occasionally until roux becomes dark brown.

Fried Okra:
Mix eggs and water in bowl. Dip okra in flour, then in eggs, then in corn flour. Deep fry at 350 degrees for 5 minutes.

Gumbo Base:
Into 2 gallon stock pot pour fish stock. Add garlic, bay leaves and thyme. Bring to boil.
Add Dark Brown Roux and allow to thicken.
Adjust heat for slow simmer.
Add dissolved file powder and simmer mixture for 1 ½ hours, skimming frequently.

Garnish/Seafood:
In a saucepan, heat salad oil. Sauté garnish ingredients at medium heat until tender.
Add seafood. Cook another 10 minutes.
Be cautious not to overcook.

Gumbo Mixture:
Add seafood and garnish to Gumbo Base.
Simmer 10 minutes more.
Add salt, pepper and cayenne to taste.

To Serve:
Serve in soup bowls. Top each portion with 3-4 pieces of Fried Okra.

Le Café

Hotel Monteleone • 214 Rue Royale • New Orleans, 70130 • Tel 504-523-3341 Ext 4262

Fortunately for the rest of the world, Café Du Monde now has several locations in Louisiana, but for me, the original location at 800 Decatur, in the French Market, is the only one. If anyone ever asks me what the first thing a newbie to New Orleans should do, I will say without hesitation, "Go to Café Du Monde for beignets and *café au lait*." Beignets are square pieces of dough, fried and blanketed with powdered sugar. Caution: Beignets are DELICIOUSLY addictive and hazardous to your health. The original Café Du Monde is open 24 hours a day, seven days a week, closed only from 6 p.m. on Christmas Eve to 6 a.m. on December 26th. The limited menu consists of dark roasted coffee with chicory, beignets, white and chocolate milk and fresh squeezed orange juice. The coffee is served black or *au lait*, i.e., mixed half and half with hot milk. Go for it!

Café Du Monde Beignets

Yield: about 2 dozen beignets

You will need:
Café Du Monde Beignet Mix*
Water
Flour
Oil for frying

Cooking Tip: *Use an electric skillet for best results.*

To Prepare:
In a bowl, stir 2 cups Beignet Mix and 7 fluid ounces water together with a spoon until blended.
On a floured surface, roll dough to 1/8" thickness, using flour liberally on dough to prevent sticking as you roll.
Cut dough into 2 ¼" squares. (You should have about 2 dozen squares.)
Pour 1"-2" of oil into skillet and heat to 370 degrees.

Cooking Tip: *Maintain proper oil temperature by cooking only a few beignets at a time; oil should remain hot enough for dough to pop to surface 8-10 seconds after it is placed in oil.*

Fry beignets in small batches, turning to cook both sides and basting continually until they are puffy and light golden brown. As beignets become done, remove them from oil and set aside to drain on paper towels.

To Serve:
Sprinkle hot beignets generously with powdered sugar and serve immediately, with a cup of CAFÉ DU MONDE CAFÉ Au-Lait.
Bon Appétit!

*For mail orders, request order blanks from Café Du Monde Coffee Stand, 1039 Decatur Street, New Orleans, Louisiana 70116; or place your order by internet at www.cafedumonde.com.

Cafe Du Monde ®
ORIGINAL FRENCH MARKET COFFEE STAND ℠
NEW ORLEANS, LA.

BEIGNET MIX
FRENCH DOUGHNUTS

(1 LB 12OZ) (793.8 g)

Café Du Monde

800 Decatur St. • New Orleans 70116 • Tel 504-525-4544

PIG WEED COCKLEBUR SICKLE

COCHON

CAJUN SOUTHERN COOKING

A lively, comfortable dining room with an open kitchen. Southern fare with a strong Cajun twist. The folks at Cochon (French for "pig") butcher all their own pigs and even prepare their own spicy vinegar and many other items "from scratch." Diners delighted with Cochon's special vinegar can even buy some to take home. Cochon enjoyed the limelight recently as a nominee for Best New Restaurant in the James Beard Foundation's annual competition. Chefs and co-owners Stephen Stryjewski and Donald Link make magic with their small plates--- Crawfish Pie, Fried Chicken Livers with Pepper Jelly Toast, Wood-Fired Oyster Roast. Entrées include Louisiana Cochon with Turnips, Cabbage and Cracklin's, Rabbit and Dumplings, Smoked Beef Brisket with Horseradish Potato Salad. Try the Cochon Mud Pie for dessert.

The Cochon Mud Pie

Yield: 12 slices

Crust:
2 cups graham cracker crumbs
¼ cup butter, softened
1 egg yolk

Filling:
1 cup light corn syrup
3 eggs
1/3 cup butter, melted
1 cup brown sugar
2 ½ cups pecan pieces

Ice Cream:
1 can sweetened condensed milk
4 egg yolks
2 cups heavy cream
½ cup whole milk
4 ounces baker's chocolate, chopped
1 tablespoon cinnamon

Marshmallow:
6 egg whites
6 ounces sugar
Water
1 sheet gelatin

Toppings:
Candied pecans
Chocolate sauce

Preheat oven to 350 degrees. Spray a 10" spring form pan with nonstick spray.

In a small bowl, combine ingredients for crust. Mix together until mixture looks like coarse crumbs. Place mixture into prepared spring form pan; distribute mixture evenly across bottom pan and press into place to form smooth crust. Bake for 15 minutes. Allow to cool completely.

In a medium bowl, combine first 4 ingredients for filling. Whisk together until smooth. Pour on top of cooled crust. Sprinkle pecan pieces evenly on top of filling. Bake again at 350 degrees until filling is set. Let cool to room temperature, then place in freezer. Filling needs to be frozen before you place the ice cream on top.

Chef's Note: *The ice cream can be prepared in any type of ice cream machine. Just follow the manufacturer's instructions for your machine.*

For the ice cream base, combine sweetened condensed milk and egg yolks in a large bowl. Place chopped chocolate in a separate bowl. Bring heavy cream and whole milk to a simmer; pour over chocolate in bowl. Stir until chocolate is completely melted. Temper the hot chocolate mixture into the eggs and condensed milk. Stir in cinnamon. Allow mixture to cool completely. Freeze mixture in ice cream machine, according to manufacturer's directions.

Take pie from freezer. Spread ice cream on top in an even layer. Return pie to freezer.

For marshmallow, place 6 ounces sugar in a small pot; add water just to dampen the sugar. Heat sugar to 236 degrees (use a candy thermometer: 236 degrees is the soft ball stage). In bowl of electric mixer with whisk attachment, whip egg whites until medium peaks form. Melt sheet of gelatin. With mixer running, add melted gelatin. Continuing to whisk, pour sugar in a slow, steady stream into the egg white mixture. Whip until stiff peaks form.

Remove pie from freezer again and place marshmallow mixture on top of the pie. Spread marshmallow mixture evenly across pie. Store completed pie in freezer.

To Serve:
Top with candied pecans and chocolate sauce.

Cochon

930 Tchoupitoulas St. • New Orleans, 70130 • Tel 504-588-2123

A classy but fun destination. Beautifully decorated indoor dining rooms; outdoor dining in good weather. Chef Tory McPhail knows his business and runs a tight ship. Go for the weekend brunch and enjoy the live Dixieland music of Joe Simon's Jazz Trio. The brunch menu is extensive. Simplify your life with the Traditional Jazz Brunch option, which starts out with a Bloody Mary and takes you all the way through dessert. Or order *á la carte* and save room for Louisiana Strawberry Shortcake: Pontchatoula strawberries on a warm buttermilk biscuit with chantilly cream and powdered sugar. Recommended in *1,000 Places in the U.S.A. and Canada to See Before You Die* (Workman Publishing, May 2007).

Dove Poppers with Five Pepper Jelly

Yield: 24 poppers

Chef's Comments:

It doesn't take long to figure out that the meal after the hunt is as important as the hunting itself. Once you see the bottles of wine, the jars of secret marinade, the favorite black cast iron skillet and little grills lugged to and unloaded at the camp, you know you're in for a serious on-the-spot meal in the awe-inspiring outdoors. Down here in Louisiana, every hunter we know makes some version of poppers at camp. Our favorite version is dove breast rolled around jalapeño slices and jack cheese, wrapped in bacon, grilled and dipped in five pepper jelly. Another version we like is made with duck, has the same fillings and is fried. You'll want to make as many of these tasty treats as you can because no one can eat just one---they're addictive and incredible with a cold beer or a shot of Tequila. By the way, they freeze well, too.

12 slices bacon, halved crosswise
24 boneless, skin-on dove breasts (double breasted)
Kosher salt and freshly ground black pepper to taste
2 ounces pepper jack cheese, sliced into thin strips
3 jalapeños, seeded and sliced into thin strips
Toothpicks
Five pepper jelly, or other spicy jelly

Preparation Tip: *Poppers ready for grilling may be covered and refrigerated for up to 2 days or frozen for up to 1 month.*

Preheat oven to 325 degrees. Lay bacon on a small baking sheet. Bake until halfway cooked, about 10 minutes. Cool bacon slightly until cool enough to handle. Season each dove on both sides with salt and pepper. Place one double breast, skin side down, on each bacon slice. On each double breast, place cheese and jalapeño strips, allowing equal amounts of filling for each popper. Fold each double breast over to enclose filling. Roll bacon strip around filled popper and secure with a toothpick.

To Grill:

Grill over moderate heat, turning occasionally, until bacon is crisp (allow about 5 minutes). Transfer poppers to a platter, remove toothpicks and let rest 5 minutes. Serve poppers with five pepper jelly for dipping.

Commander's Palace

1403 Washington Ave. • New Orleans 70130 • Tel 504-899-8221

Located on the spot where sisters Emma and Bertha Camors operated a notions shop for many years, starting in 1886, The Court of Two Sisters was named in honor of these aristocratic Creole ladies who sold clothing, lace and perfumes imported from Paris. The courtyard itself is possibly the largest restaurant courtyard in town. And of the many jazz brunch buffets offered in this city of good food and good music, the buffet at The Court of Two Sisters may be the most massive display of Creole, Cajun and French dishes of them all. If you love the sight of a grand feast, one look at this bounty may take your breath away. Old World charm, gorgeous flowering plants in season, the gently gurgling courtyard fountains. No wonder *New Orleans Magazine* readers chose The Court of Two Sisters in their "Best Courtyard Dining" category; a *Where Magazine* survey of U.S. and international visitors honored the restaurant with a "Best Dining – Gold Award." Jazz Brunch Buffet daily. Creole A La Carte Dinner, Monday through Saturday.

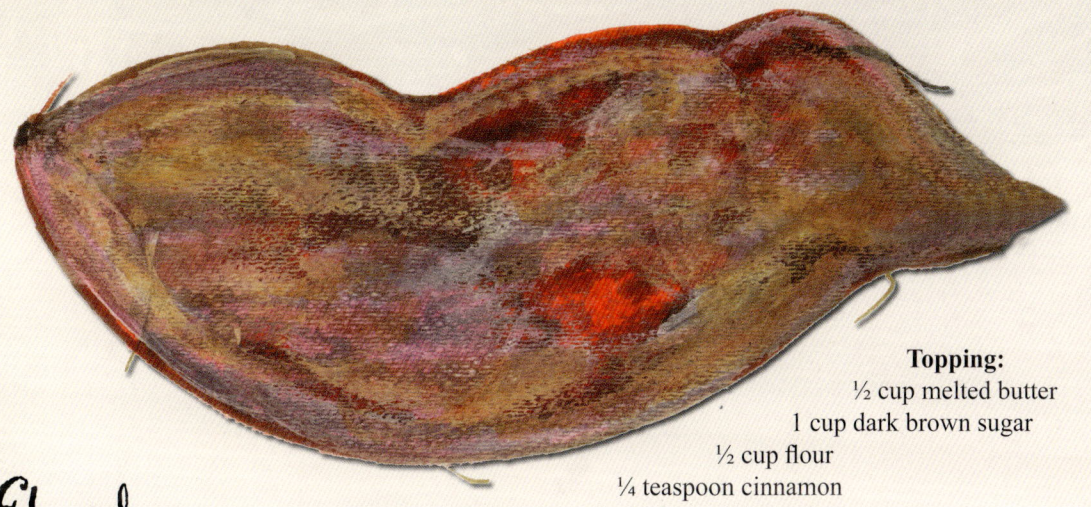

Glazed Sweet Potatoes

Yield: 10-12 servings

Base:
½ cup melted butter
½ cup sugar
2 eggs, beaten
1 teaspoon vanilla
1/3 cup milk
6 cups sweet potatoes, peeled, cut into
  1" cubes, steamed and cooled

Method:
Preheat oven to 350 degrees. Combine butter, sugar, eggs, vanilla and milk in mixing bowl and stir well. Fold in sweet potatoes. Pour mixture into a 2-quart casserole dish and top with Topping (see below). Bake at 350 degrees for 20-25 minutes.

Topping:
½ cup melted butter
1 cup dark brown sugar
½ cup flour
¼ teaspoon cinnamon
1 pinch nutmeg
1 cup pecans, chopped

Method:
Combine all ingredients in mixing bowl and stir well.

Seafood Orleans Omelet

Yield: 4 individual omelets

Seafood Orleans Base:
(enough for 4 omelets)
3 ounces butter
½ cup red onions, julienned
½ cup red bell peppers, julienned
½ cup green bell peppers, julienned
1 tablespoon garlic, minced
½-1 pound 31-35 count shrimp, peeled and deveined
3 ounces sherry
½-1 pound crawfish tails
½-1 pound jumbo lump crabmeat
2 teaspoons Creole seasoning
1 cup heavy cream
¼ cup green onions, tops only, sliced thin
1 tablespoon parsley, chopped fine

Method:
Heat butter in a large sauté skillet on medium heat. Add red onions, both bell peppers and garlic; cook until soft. Add shrimp and cook until they start to turn pink. Add sherry and reduce liquid by 2/3. Add crawfish tails, crabmeat, Creole seasoning and cream; reduce by 2/3. Stir in green onions and parsley. Set aside and keep warm.

For Each Individual Seafood Orleans Omelet:
1 tablespoon butter or margarine
3 eggs, beaten
1 pinch salt
1 portion of Seafood Orleans Base (i.e., ¼ of above recipe per individual omelet)

Garnish for Each Omelet:
1 orange slice
1 sprig parsley

Method for Each Omelet:
Heat butter or margarine in omelet skillet on medium heat. Add 3 beaten eggs. As the sides cook, use a rubber spatula to pull the firm edges toward the middle of the pan and let the egg run under and toward the edges (this will fluff the omelet). When omelet is ¾ of the way cooked, flip it over and cook the other side. When omelet is cooked through, spoon a quarter of the Seafood Orleans Base onto the center and gently fold the omelet in half over the filling. Garnish with an orange slice and a parsley sprig.

The Court of Two Sisters

613 Rue Royale • New Orleans 70130 • Tel 504-522-7261

A small French neighborhood bistro in Uptown, at streetcar stop #27, La Crêpe Nanou serves the best mussels around. Mussel enthusiasts, simply think, "La Crêpe Nanou." I myself fell in love with the superbly seasoned French Onion Soup. Yum! Among the entrées, look for Sautéed Sweetbreads topped with capers in lemon butter sauce, Roasted Leg of Lamb topped with Cognac sauce and served with garlic mixed vegetables and potatoes or Grilled Quail topped with mushroom sauce and served with garlic mixed vegetables and angel hair pasta. Dessert as the French might have it: delicate, delicious crêpes, quite sinful. La Crêpe Nanou is closed Sunday and Monday.

French Onion Soup

Yield: 10 servings

8 whole onions (4 pounds)
1 tablespoon minced garlic
½ teaspoon black pepper
1 tablespoon olive oil or bacon fat
4 bay leaves
4 quarts chicken stock
½ teaspoon chicken base
½ teaspoon beef base
10 slices baked French bread
20 ounces shredded Gruyère cheese
Salt to taste

Slice onions.
In soup pot, cook onions in olive oil or bacon fat on high flame for 7-10 minutes.
Reduce heat to low and, stirring occasionally, allow mixture to simmer for 1 hour, or until onions are tender and brown.
Add chicken stock, garlic, black pepper and bay leaves to soup pot. Bring to boil.
Add chicken and beef base to soup, then salt to taste.

To serve:
Ladle portions of soup into individual, heat resistant soup bowls.
In each bowl, place a slice of baked bread; top bread with shredded Gruyère.
Place bowls of soup under broiler and heat until cheese/bread topping turns golden brown.

Steamed Mussels

Yield: 1 large serving or 2 small servings

1 pound washed mussels
2 ounces chopped onion
¼ teaspoon thyme
1 cup white wine
1 tablespoon heavy cream
1 tablespoon olive oil
1 tablespoon minced parsley/crushed garlic mixture

Heat olive oil in pot on high flame.
Add onions and thyme and sauté for 1½ minutes.
Add mussels and wine; cover with tight fitting lid.
After about 2 minutes of cooking, as soon as steam begins to escape the pot, begin checking to see if mussels are open.
When most of the mussels are open, add heavy cream and the parsley/garlic mixture to the pot. Discard any mussels that have failed to open.
Gently stir the open mussels and the sauce together. Serve at once.

La Crêpe Nanou Restaurant

1410 Rue Robert • New Orleans 70115 • Tel 504-899-2670

Walking into Rose and Gerard Marchal's pastry shop is routine with me and always a pleasant experience. I can count on seeing Rose's smiling face at the register. Fresh French pastries and quiches of all kinds. Most often, I order the Quiche Lorraine. If I must have something sweet, the decision takes a while as I stand at the glass counter, hoping the next person in line is a patient sort. Carrot muffins, apple strudel, Napoleon fruit tarts, almond croissants, cheese Danishes, brioches, strawberry shortcake and mango mousse. During Mardi Gras, King Cakes rule, plain or filled with cream cheese, lemon, raspberry or apple. Open Wednesday through Sunday, 7 a.m. to 2 p.m.

Anise Brioche

Yield: 10 individual brioches

1 pound flour
4-5 eggs for dough
Pinch of salt
3 ounces sugar
½ teaspoon dry yeast
½ pound butter
1 teaspoon anise seeds
Zest of ½ lemon
1 egg for egg wash

With mixer on 1st speed, mix flour, salt, sugar and dry yeast for 1 minute.
Add eggs and mix for 5 minutes more.
Mix in butter a little at a time until well incorporated.
Add anise seeds and lemon zest; mix for 2 more minutes.
Let dough rest at room temperature for 1 hour.

Gently fold dough into a ball and refrigerate overnight.

The next day, cut dough into 10 equal size pieces. Shape pieces into balls and let rest for 40 minutes at room temperature.

Beat egg for egg wash and brush tops of the 10 brioches.

Preheat oven to 350 degrees.
Bake brioches for 18-20 minutes, until golden brown.

Chef's Comment: *"Perfect with foie gras"*

Orange Cranberry Pound Cake

3 ounces sugar + 3 ounces orange zest (mix together in food processor)
8 ounces butter, softened
5 ounces sugar
4-5 eggs
½ lemon zest
8 ounces flour
Pinch of baking soda

Preheat oven to 350 degrees.
In mixing bowl, mix sugar and butter for 5 minutes. Gradually add eggs.
Beat for 5 minutes. Reduce mixing speed to and add flour, baking soda, sugar and orange mixture.
Beat 3 minutes.
Add cranberries and beat for 2 minutes.
Pour batter into a greased baking loaf pan.
Bake for 30-35 minutes.

Croissant d'Or Patisserie

617 Ursulines Ave. • New Orleans 70116 • Tel 504-524-4663

ELEVEN79

Est. 2000

In 2005, the Hurricane Katrina disaster led to the closing of Eleven79 by then owner S. Joseph Segreto. Joe Segreto went on to become the mastermind behind The Inn at Hunt Phelan, a now highly regarded restaurant in Memphis. As New Orleans moved toward recovery in 2006, Eleven79 proudly re-opened. The décor is classic: lots of dark wood and exposed brick. Taste-test the large Vetrano olives from Sicily offered at the bar. I was sorely tempted to park myself at the bar, directly in front of the Vetrano olives. I was able to resist only because the magnificent table of antipasto trays caught my attention. A table in the bar, used for dining on weekends, is reserved for antipasto trays on weekdays. Chef James Sibel creates Italian-Creole masterpieces: Veal Fiorentina, Pasta Acciuga, Roast Duck Arancia, Babbalucci Sfogliatta, Ossobucco Milanese. Of course, the dessert menu includes a mouth-watering Tiramisu. Open Monday through Saturday for dinner. Tasty lunch specials Thursday and Friday only.

Southern Style Cheesecake

3 pounds cream cheese
14 ounces sugar
2 cups buttermilk
2 cups sour cream
6 whole eggs
4 egg yolks
1 tablespoon vanilla
1 cup unsalted butter
3 cups graham cracker crumbs

Filling:
Whip cheese and sugar in stand mixer with paddle attachment until light and airy.
Add buttermilk and sour cream; mix well.
Add vanilla; then with mixer on low speed, add whole eggs and egg yolks one at a time and mix until just incorporated. Do not over mix.

Crust:
Melt butter and add to graham cracker crumbs.
Mix well. Line bottom and sides of a 10" spring form pan with a thin layer of the butter/crumb mixture.

Completion:
Pour batter into crust.
Wrap cake pan in foil and place in baking dish with 2" of water.
Bake at 350 degrees for 2 hours, or until middle is firm and the top is puffy and light golden brown in color.
Let cool at room temperature for 30 minutes.
Refrigerate for 4 hours or until set.

Pasta Chiumenzana

3 Roma tomatoes
1 pint cherry tomatoes
1 pint grape tomatoes
2 tablespoons sugar
¾ cup fresh basil
1 ½ tablespoons crushed red pepper flakes
3 14-ounce cans whole peeled plum tomatoes
½ cup olive oil
Salt and pepper to taste

Cooked pasta of your choice

Grated Romano cheese to taste
Additional fresh basil for garnish

To Prepare Sauce:
Slice Roma tomatoes into ¼-inch rounds and set aside.
Add to the Roma tomatoes half of the cherry tomatoes and half of the grape tomatoes.
Cut each of the remaining cherry and grape tomatoes in half and add them to the fresh tomato mixture.
Pour olive oil into pan and heat until almost smoking.
Add fresh tomato mixture, red pepper flakes, sugar, salt and pepper.
Cook over medium heat for 15-20 minutes.
Add canned tomatoes and cook for 25-30 minutes more.
Remove pan from heat. Tear basil into strips by hand and add to pot.
Check seasoning and adjust if necessary.

To Serve:
For each pound of cooked pasta being served, heat 2 cups sauce in sauté pan.
As soon as sauce reaches boiling, add cooked pasta and cook just until pasta is heated through.
Remove pan from heat immediately to avoid overcooking.
Garnish with fresh basil and grated Romano cheese.

Eleven79

1179 Annunciation St. • New Orleans 70119 • Tel 504-299-1179

What goes on behind the dark brown awnings on St. Charles Avenue? I was really curious. After all, Emeril's Delmonico has received enough fanfare to intimidate the most intrepid foodie. Upon entering, I found two very tall velvety couches on either side of a glass top table. Velvet drapes and piano music. Very cool. Everything tastefully done, especially the food. What could beat the Jumbo Lump Crabmeat Cake with Mango Butter and Cucumbers Kimchi? What about Roasted Mediterranean Branzino with Fennel Purée, Marinated Tomatoes, Pancetta, Lemon Confit and Black Olive Oil? The Bone-in Ribeye was the best steak I've ever eaten. Dry aged for 21 days. I'm totally spoiled. Classic New Orleans Creole cuisine, reinvented for the contemporary palate. Reservations strongly recommended. Complimentary valet parking offered in front of the restaurant.

Trout Delmonico*

Makes 4 servings

Chef's Comments: *This signature dish from the La Franca's Delmonico tenure is a celebration of local seafood, with large trout fillets topped by shrimp and oysters and lemon butter sauce---simple, elegant, and delicious.*

4 tablespoons unsalted butter, melted
1 tablespoon fresh lemon juice
½ teaspoon plus 1/8 teaspoon salt
½ teaspoon plus 1/8 teaspoon freshly ground white
  pepper
Four 7- to 8-ounce trout fillets
12 medium shrimp, peeled and deveined
12 medium oysters, drained
1 teaspoon chopped fresh parsley
4 fresh parsley sprigs, for garnish
4 lemon wedges, for garnish
4 tomato wedges, for garnish

Preheat the oven to 350 degrees F. Line a large baking sheet with parchment paper.

Combine the melted butter, lemon juice, 1/8 teaspoon of salt, and 1/8 teaspoon of the white pepper in a small bowl.

Arrange the fish on the baking sheet without touching and place 3 shrimp on top of each fillet, spacing them about 1-inch apart. Using a pastry brush, lightly coat the tops of the fillets and the shrimp with the lemon-butter mixture and season each with 1/8 teaspoon of the remaining salt and 1/8 teaspoon of the remaining white pepper. Bake, basting twice with the lemon-butter mixture, until the fish is opaque and the shrimp are just pink, 8 to 10 minutes.

Remove the fish from the oven. Increase the heat to broil and move the top rack to the highest position. Place 3 oysters on top of each fillet, alternating with the shrimp. Brush the fish, shrimp, and oysters with the remaining lemon-butter mixture, sprinkle each fillet with ¼ teaspoon of the parsley, and broil until the edges of the oysters begin to curl, 3 to 4 minutes. Arrange one fillet on each of 4 serving plates. Garnish the plates with the fresh parsley sprigs, and lemon and tomato wedges, and serve immediately.

*Recipe courtesy Emeril Lagasse, Emeril's Delmonico: A Restaurant with a Past, *William Morrow Publishers, 2005*

Emeril's Delmonico Restaurant

1300 St. Charles Ave. • New Orleans 70130 • Tel 504-525-4937

FEELINGS CAFE
RESTAURANT AND PATIO LOUNGE

Feelings is tucked away in New Orleans' historic Faubourg Marigny. During the tenure of founding owners Les Carloss and Bud Deslatte, Chef Sylvia Harbin's Peanut Butter Pie became Feelings' trademark dessert. Former Feelings co-owner Les Carloss now serves Peanut Butter Pie as "Cajun Velvet Pie" at Bluff City Bayou in Memphis. About Bluff City Bayou's Cajun Velvet (a.k.a. Peanut Butter Pie at Feelings), *Bon Appétit* has noted, it's "worth the trip to the restaurant by itself." Feelings current co-owners Jim Baird and Dale deBruyne proudly serve Peanut Butter Pie and sensational Creole specialties. Live piano music in the Patio Bar most weekends. Noteworthy: The lovely deBruyne Guest House New Orleans, owned by Dale, sits across the street from the restaurant and boasts a swimming pool, a significant amenity on a hot day.

Feelings Café
Seafood Eggplant

Yield: 8-10 servings

½ cup chopped onion
½ cup chopped bell pepper
½ cup chopped celery
12 ounces butter
6 cups peeled, cubed eggplant
2 cups cooked rice
1 tablespoon Italian seasoning
1 tablespoon Tabasco
½ cup finely chopped green onion
1 pound crawfish tails
4 cups peeled, deveined shrimp
Salt and pepper to taste

Additional ingredients:
1 slice fried eggplant per serving
Hollandaise sauce
Sliced green onions for garnish

In large pan, sauté onion, bell pepper and celery in
12 ounces butter.
Add cubed eggplant and chopped sausage to mixture
and cook until sausage is browned.
Add cooked rice, Italian seasoning, Tabasco and
finely chopped green onion; cook until heated
through.
Add crawfish and shrimp; simmer briefly, removing
from heat when seafood is cooked.   Season with
salt and pepper to taste.

To plate:
Place a slice of fried eggplant on each plate.
Ladle a serving of Seafood Eggplant over the fried
eggplant.
Top with warm Hollandaise sauce and garnish with
sliced green onions.

Feelings Café
House Dressing,
Poppy Seed Vinaigrette

3 tablespoons dry mustard
3 tablespoons warm water
½ cup puréed onions
1 cup white vinegar
1 ½ cups olive oil
1 ½ teaspoons salt
4 ½ tablespoons sugar
1 ½ tablespoons poppy seed

Combine dry mustard and warm water in a bowl; put
aside.
Purée onion in blender.
Blend vinegar, sugar and salt into pureed onions.
With blender still running, slowly drizzle olive oil into
mixture.
Add mustard and water mixture to blender and pulse.
Finally, stir poppy seeds into dressing.
Refrigerate for several hours before serving.

Feelings Café

Celebrating over 100 years of excellence, Galatoire's is the prototypical New Orleans restaurant. This *grande dame* is the proud recipient of numerous awards, too many to list here. Brilliant white starched tablecloths, bentwood chairs, ceiling fans with brass hardware, polished brass light fixtures and coat hooks, old style water bottles. Galatoire's stands for tradition, no doubt about that. A few items from the menu of classics: Fried Eggplant and Soufflé Potatoes Bearnaise, Shrimp Remoulade, Crabmeat Sardou, Chicken Clemenceau, Brabant Potatoes, Oysters en Brochette, Poisson Meunière Amandine. Friday lunches are perhaps most popular with locals, who often make an entire afternoon of the meal. Open Tuesday through Sunday. Jackets required for dinner; jackets all day on Sunday.

Jackson Soup

Yield: about 1 ½ gallons, or 8-10 servings

Chef's Comments: *The delicate flavor of the leeks is enhanced when the soup is made a day in advance, chilled and reheated before serving. A glass of Chablis and a hunk of warm, crusty French bread are the perfect accompaniments. This soup will keep for four days in the refrigerator and a month in the freezer.*

Salt to taste
9 large baking potatoes, peeled and cut into medium dice
2 leeks, cleaned and finely diced (white and green parts)
1 ½ pounds smoked ham, cut into medium dice
2 cups whole milk
2 cups all-purpose flour
Freshly ground white pepper to taste

Pour 1 ½ gallons of water into a stockpot and season with salt. Add the potatoes to the water and bring mixture to a boil. Reduce heat to medium and cook potatoes at a low rolling boil for 5 minutes. Stir in leeks and ham. Continue to cook at low rolling boil for 10 minutes, or until potatoes are soft. In mixing bowl, make a cold roux by whisking milk and flour together until smooth.
Add cold roux a little at a time to the simmering soup, stirring continuously. Cook over medium heat about 20 minutes, or until soup has thickened. Season to taste with salt and white pepper.

Shrimp Clemenceau

Yield: 6 servings

Chef's Comments*: This unusual combination is an absolute favorite among Galatoire's patrons, many of whom enjoy it with a crisp white wine such as Pouilly Fuisse. Do not attempt to "dress up" the dish by using fresh or frozen green peas instead of the canned petit pois called for here. The fancy stuff simply does not work. Stick to the easy way.*

Oil, for frying
3 baking potatoes, about 10 ounces each, peeled and cut into 3/4 " squares
Salt and freshly ground black pepper to taste
3 tablespoons salted butter
6 dozen large (21-25 count) shrimp
3 cups sliced button mushrooms
3 tablespoons minced garlic
2 cups canned peas (petit pois)

In a heavy bottomed pot suitable for frying, heat oil to 350 degrees.
Fry the potatoes in 2 batches, moving pieces around with a slotted spoon to ensure even browning. Cook for 7-9 minutes, until golden brown. Using a slotted spoon, transfer potatoes from oil to a platter lined with paper towels. Sprinkle potatoes with salt and pepper and set aside in a warm place.
Melt butter in a large sauté pan over high heat. Sauté shrimp for 3-4 minutes, until they turn pink. Add mushrooms and sauté 2-3 minutes more, until they are tender. Add garlic and peas and sauté 2-3 minutes, until peas are thoroughly heated. Season with salt and pepper. Add potatoes to pan and toss to incorporate. Distribute the Shrimp Clemenceau equally among 6 plates and serve immediately.

Galatoire's

209 Bourbon St. • New Orleans 70130 • Tel 504-525-2021

Herbsaint shouts delicious, non-traditional Southern Louisiana fare. *The New York Times, Food and Wine, Gourmet, Continental Magazine, New Orleans Magazine, USA Today* and *The Times-Picayune* have all sat up and paid attention to Chef Donald Link's culinary achievements at Herbsaint. Most recently, the James Beard Foundation named Chef Link as Best Chef: South, for 2007. At Herbsaint, the "small plates" get my vote. These give diners opportunity to try a variety of dishes in a single meal. Just a few choices: Beef Short Ribs on Potato Cake with Dijon-Horseradish Dressing, Fried Frog Legs with Fresh Fine Herbs, Shrimp and Green Chili Grits Cakes with Tasso Cream Sauce. *New Orleans Magazine* reports that the Chocolate Beignets are a favorite dessert. Indeed, Chocolate Beignets are a first-rate choice. Another top pick is my personal favorite, the Coconut Cream Pie. Lunch: Monday through Friday, 11:30 a.m. to 1:30 p.m. Dinner: Monday through Saturday, 5:30 p.m. to 10:00 p.m.

Coconut Cream Pie

Yield: Two 9" pies

Time: 1 hour, plus 2 ½ hours for chilling

For Pastry Cream:
3 cups heavy cream
½ vanilla bean, split
1 cup sugar
¼ cup cornstarch
5 large egg yolks

For Macadamia Nut Crust:
8 ounces macadamia nuts, toasted and cooled
1 cup flour
9 tablespoons butter
½ cup sugar
1 large egg yolk
½ teaspoon salt

For Assembly:
4 cups heavy cream
½ cup sugar
2 ½ cups unsweetened coconut, lightly toasted and
  cooled

Pastry Cream:
In a medium heavy bottomed saucepan, combine 2 ½ cups heavy cream and scrapings from the vanilla bean; discard the vanilla bean. In a small bowl, combine sugar and cornstarch. In a medium bowl, combine egg yolks with remaining ½ cup of cream.

Place saucepan with heavy cream and vanilla scrapings over medium heat to warm. Caution: Mixture should warm over flame, but should not reach the boiling point.

When vanilla cream in saucepan is about to boil, there will be slight movement in the pan. As the vanilla cream reaches the boiling point, whisk a few hot spoonfuls of vanilla cream into the egg yolk mixture to temper it. Reduce heat to medium low. Pour yolk mixture, now slightly warmed, into pan, stirring constantly with a wooden spoon until the mixture is thick.

Chef's Tip: *If mixture separates, transfer it to a mixer with a whisk attachment and beat until blended.*

Transfer the mixture to a shallow container. Cover with plastic wrap to keep a skin from forming on the surface. Refrigerate until cold and firm, at least 1 hour.

Macadamia Nut Crust:
Combine nuts and flour in a food processor. Process until nuts are finely ground, pulsing to keep them from becoming pasty. In mixer with paddle attachment, cream butter with sugar. Add yolk and mix thoroughly. Add nut and flour mixture, along with salt, to butter, sugar and yolk mixture. Mix until smooth. Wrap in plastic wrap and refrigerate until well chilled, about 1 hour.

Divide dough in half. Roll out one half between two sheets of plastic wrap to make a 10" disk. Repeat with remaining dough. Line two 9" tart pans with dough. Chill in freezer until very firm, about 30 minutes.

Preheat oven to 350 degrees. Place pie weights in shells and bake until lightly golden, about 15 minutes. Remove pie weights and continue to bake until crusts are golden brown, 10-15 minutes more. Allow to cool.

To Assemble:
In bowl of mixer fitted with a whisk attachment, combine heavy cream, sugar and 2 cups of pastry cream. (Reserve any remaining cream for another use.) Whisk at high speed until soft peaks form. Add coconut and continue whisking mixture by hand until very stiff. Spoon into cooled tart shells.

To Serve:
Serve immediately or refrigerate to chill.

Herbsaint Bar and Restaurant

701 St. Charles Ave. • New Orleans 70130 • Tel 504-524-4114

Irene's Cuisine: a dining destination for top-notch classic Creole-Italian food. Locals make up perhaps 80% of the clientele at this bustling and popular restaurant. They might prefer to keep Irene's to themselves, but the buzz over Irene's is way loud. Irene's is a little off the beaten tourist track, but take my advice and seek this place out. Restaurant owner Irene DiPietro presides over three romantic, dimly lit dining rooms. Irene's son, Chef Nicholas DiPietro, rules supreme in the kitchen. Out of that kitchen come Creole-Italian dishes that amaze and delight Irene's devoted patrons. You haven't died and gone to heaven until you've tried the Crabmeat Gratin. The Veal Marsala is a sure thing, as is the Chicken Rosemarino. Food-Speak at Irene's is fluent Italian with a slight Lousiana accent. Live piano music in the bar. Open for dinner Monday through Saturday. Limited number of reservations accepted.

Chicken Rosemarino

Yield: 2-3 servings

Chicken, approximately 5 pounds, cut into serving pieces

Marinade:
2 teaspoons salt
½ tablespoon cracked black pepper
½ tablespoon garlic powder
½ tablespoon dried thyme
½ tablespoon dried oregano
¼ cup extra virgin olive oil
½ cup canola oil
Juice of ½ lemon
½ cup fresh rosemary
¾ cup fresh crushed garlic

Liquids for Basting:
¾ cup low sodium chicken broth
¼ cup dry white wine

Initial preparation, one day ahead:
Rinse chicken pieces well and pat dry. Place chicken in a large zip lock bag.

In a small bowl, mix ingredients for marinade.
Pour marinade into bag over chicken.
Squeeze all air from bag and seal bag securely.
Shake sealed bag until chicken pieces are thoroughly coated with marinade.

Place sealed bag of chicken in refrigerator to marinate overnight.

Roasting procedure:
Preheat oven to 500 degrees.

Heat a large ovenproof skillet over burner and pour enough marinade from chicken to coat bottom of pan. Place a small batch of chicken pieces in skillet, skin-side down, and brown on both sides. When chicken pieces turn golden brown on both sides and are still pink in the middle, remove from pan and set aside. Repeat process until all chicken pieces have been browned.

Arrange seared chicken pieces skin-side up in skillet. Pour over them the remaining marinade, the chicken stock and the white wine.

Place skillet in preheated oven to roast chicken pieces. After initial 10 minutes of roasting, test chicken for doneness every three minutes. Remove from oven as soon as chicken is cooked all the way through. Expect roasting to require approximately 15 to 20 minutes, total.

Irene's Cuisine

539 St. Philip St. • New Orleans 70116 • Tel 504-529-8811

Is that chef in the kitchen really playing a washboard? *Mais non*, that's a *vest frottoir*! Half the chefs are playing zydeco rubboards, percussion instruments that look like washboards to the untrained eye. K-Paul's is a high energy, fun place to enjoy the tip-top-of-the-line in Southern Louisiana food. Executive Chef Paul Miller hails from Opelousas, Louisiana, as does Chef Paul Prudhomme, celebrity chef, cookbook author and founding magician of K-Paul's. Chef Paul and Executive Chef Miller work closely together to operate K-Paul's Kitchen as well as to consult in the U.S. and abroad, to develop new products, to support training programs for chefs and to share K-Paul's Louisiana cuisine with the world through catering. Catering motto: "The Best Food on Earth, Anywhere on the Planet." After Hurricane Katrina, the chefs touched many people's lives by feeding storm survivors for free out of their kitchen. My son, a chef, has commented, "New Orleans cuisine is epitomized in the food of K-Paul's."

Bronzed Fish

Yield: 4 servings

Chef's Note: *Bronzing is a wonderful cooking technique for meat or fish---and it's so simple. You can actually roast one side of the meat or fish at a time on a heavy griddle or in a large, heavy aluminum skillet or electric skillet heated to 350 degrees. (You can purchase a surface thermometer, or pyrometer, to measure dry temperature of griddle or aluminum skillet.) If you omit butter stages, bronzing produces delicious reduced-fat meat and fish dishes. Simply spray fish or meat surfaces with nonstick cooking spray just before applying seasoning.*

3 tablespoons unsalted butter, melted, or oil
4 fish fillets, 4 ½ ounces each, about ½ to ¾ thick at
   thickest part
1 tablespoon plus 1 teaspoon of **one** of the following
   seasonings:
     Chef Paul Prudhomme's Seafood Magic®
     Blackened Redfish Magic®
     Meat Magic®
     Shrimp Magic®
     Fajita Magic®
     Salmon Magic®
     Magic Seasoning Salt®
     Magic Salt-Free Seasoning®
     Barbecue Magic®

Place a nonstick skillet over medium high heat until hot, about 7 minutes.
Lightly coat both sides of each fillet with butter, then sprinkle one side with ½ teaspoon of the seasoning of your choice. Place fish in heated skillet, seasoned sides down. Sprinkle top sides of fillets evenly with remaining seasoning.

Cook until undersides of fillets are bronze in color, about 2 ½ minutes. Watch as fish cooks, and you'll see a white line coming up the side of each fillet as it turns from translucent to opaque. When ½ of the thickness is opaque, the fillet is ready to be turned. Turn each fillet as it becomes ready, and cook about 2 ½ minutes longer.

To test for doneness, simply touch fillet in center: properly cooked fillet will have stiffer texture than partially cooked fish. You can also use a fork to flake fillet at its thickest part: if it flakes easily, it is done. **Serve immediately,** with Jalapeño Tartar Sauce (recipe below).

Cooking Tips:
Be aware that even after you remove fish from the heat, it will continue to cook briefly. **Do not overcook.** *You can turn the fillets more than once, or even continuously, until they are done.* **<u>All cooking times are approximate.</u>**

Jalapeño Tartar Sauce

Yield: about 1 ½ cups

1 cup Hellman's® brand mayonnaise
1 tablespoon green jalapeño chilies, finely diced
2 teaspoons red jalapeño chilies, finely diced
½ teaspoon lemon juice
2 tablespoons horseradish sauce
2 tablespoons red onion, finely diced
2 tablespoons green bell peppers, finely diced
¼ cup sweet pickle relish
1 teaspoon garlic, minced
2 hard boiled eggs, shelled and finely diced
1 teaspoon Chef Paul Prudhomme's Vegetable Magic®
1 teaspoon Chef Paul Prudhomme's Barbecue Magic®
1 teaspoon Chef Paul Prudhomme's Magic Pepper
   Sauce®

Combine all ingredients in a food processor and pulse until well blended. Refrigerate until ready to use.

K-Paul's Louisiana Kitchen

Not in New Orleans, Latil's Landing is well worth the drive (45 minutes to 1 hour) to its home at Houmas House Plantation and Gardens, near Darrow, Louisiana. The restaurant's gifted Executive Chef Jeremy Langlois progressed quickly as a student at the Chef John Folse Culinary Institute of Nicholls State University in Thibodaux, Louisiana. At age 22, he became the youngest executive chef of any restaurant in DiRoNA, an organization of 750 premier restaurants in the U.S., Canada and Mexico. Dining Langlois style educates the palate. *Chez* Langlois, expect unpredictable yet wildly successful combinations of flavors. A few menu items: Crab and Mango Cake, Sweet Potato Gnocchi, Black Drum Sam, Lobster and Creole Tomato Risotto, Rack of Lamb Burnside and Breast of Duck. The dessert menu---a great read! How to settle on just one dessert? White Chocolate and Coconut Bread Pudding, Chocolate Paté, Peanut Butter Cheesecake. Named one of the Top 20 Restaurants in America by *Esquire Magazine*.

Corn Maque Choux

Yield: 6 servings

Ingredients:

8 ears fresh corn
¼ cup andouille sausage, finely diced
½ cup bacon drippings
1 cup onion, chopped
½ cup celery, chopped
½ cup green bell pepper, chopped
½ cup red bell pepper, chopped
¼ cup garlic, diced
2 cups tomatoes, coarsely chopped
2 tablespoons tomato sauce
1 cup green onions, sliced
Salt and black pepper to taste

Method:

Select tender, well developed ears of corn.
Remove shucks and silk. Using a sharp
knife, cut lengthwise through the kernels to
remove them from the cob. Scrape each cob,
using the blade of the knife to remove all milk
and additional pulp from the corn.
In a cast iron Dutch oven, melt bacon drippings
over medium high heat. Sauté corn, onions, celery,
bell peppers, garlic and andouille about 15-20 minutes,
or until vegetables are wilted and corn begins to become
tender. Add tomatoes and tomato sauce. Continue
cooking until juice from tomatoes is rendered into the
dish, approximately 15-20 minutes. Add green onions
and season to taste with salt and pepper. Continue to
cook an additional 15 minutes.

Perfect Onion Rings

Yield: 4 servings

Chef's Comments: *Onion rings are one of my all time
favorites. I have spent a great deal of time to perfect them
and have tried many different techniques to prepare them.
But, thanks to some of the great chefs that I work with, they
have let me know the secrets to making this recipe just right.
Thank you, Taylor Francies, Clover Lucan and Ross Ford
for showing me the way.*

1 cup milk
¼ cup hot sauce
2 large yellow onions, peeled and cut into
  1/8" thick rings
1 ½ cups all-purpose flour
½ cup cornmeal
Salt and pepper to taste
Vegetable oil for frying

In a bowl, combine the milk with the hot sauce. Season
to taste with salt and pepper. Add onion rings and press
to coat. Marinate, covered, in refrigerator for at least 1 hour.
To a medium pot, add 2" of oil. Heat oil to 360 degrees. In
a shallow bowl, combine flour and cornmeal. Season to
taste with salt and pepper. Dredge the marinated onion
rings in seasoned flour mixture, coating each ring
evenly. Shake off any excess flour.
Fry the onion rings in batches, placing them carefully in the
hot oil and turning to cook evenly and to prevent sticking.
As the onion rings turn golden brown, remove them from
the oil and place on paper towels to drain. Each batch
should require about 3 minutes to cook.

Latil's Landing Restaurant

Houmas House Plantation and Gardens • 40136 Highway 942 • Darrow, LA 70725-2302 • Tel 1-888-323-8314

L üke opened in May 2007 and is well on its way to becoming a roaring success. Chef John Besh, winner of the 2006 James Beard Award for Best Chef: Southeast, describes Lüke as "Alsace meets New Orleans" with French, German, Jewish and Creole influences. Diners can observe Chef Jared Tees and his staff at work in the open kitchen. Menu items are innovative; some ingredients are organic. My breakfast choice: two organic poached eggs over crab cakes, artisan country ham and blood orange Hollandaise. At lunch, I loved Lüke's terrific matzo ball and roast chicken soup, which would be a hit even with my favorite Jewish cousin, a true connoisseur of chicken soups. Anytime, from the Raw Bar: lobster, crab, oysters, shrimp, prawns, mussels, clams, langoustines. Hours: 7 a.m. to 11 p.m. daily.

"BLT" Buster Crab, Lettuce and Tomato Sandwich

Yield: 4 servings

For Crab:
8 buster crabs, cleaned
1 cup cornmeal
1 cup seasoned flour
Canola oil, for frying (about 1 quart)
Salt and pepper to taste

For Aioli:
4 egg yolks
1 head garlic, minced
2 cups canola oil

Sandwich Assembly:
1 head Bibb lettuce
1 pound Benton's Smoked Country Bacon, thickly
  sliced
8 slices white Pullman bread
Butter
2 Creole tomatoes, sliced
Salt and pepper to taste

Method:
In a sauté pan, heat canola oil over medium high flame, in preparation for frying. Season buster crabs with salt and pepper. Mix cornmeal and seasoned flour; toss buster crabs in mixture, to coat.

Place buster crabs in hot canola oil and cook 1 ½ minutes on each side. Remove from oil and set aside on paper towels to drain.

Spread butter on each slice of Pullman bread; toast bread on griddle.

Cook bacon until crisp. Set aside on paper towels to drain.

To make the aioli, emulsify 4 egg yolks, minced garlic and 2 cups canola oil. Season to taste with salt. Season tomatoes with salt and pepper.

To Plate:
Spread aioli generously on each slice of toast. Arrange two slices of toast on a plate. On one slice of toast, place portions of Bibb lettuce, bacon and tomatoes. On the other slice of toast, place 2 buster crabs. Serve with *pommes frites.*

333 St. Charles Ave. • New Orleans 70130 • Tel 504-378-2840

mélange

Mélange serves classic New Orleans dishes made from recipes developed at renowned area restaurants: Mélange brings you the best of the Crescent City's best, all in one location. Additionally, the menu includes noteworthy original dishes created by Mélange's talented culinary team. I was graciously welcomed and seated. In the blink of an eye, a serving of fresh-from-the-oven bruschetta topped with fresh garlic, Parmesan and tomato appeared before me. The fun was just beginning. Check out the Grilled Scallops, the Chopped Portobello Mushrooms and the Oyster and Brie Bisque. Exquisite. Mélange may offer the most extensive wine list by the glass in the Tri-State Area. The décor is elegant and sophisticated, with handsome rosy hardwood floors. Candles and a rose on every table. Extraordinary service and live N'awlins jazz. Mélange is a first class operation in every respect.

Louisiana Crab Cake

Yield: 1 serving

Moque Choux Preparation:

2 ounces diced tomato
2 ounces corn kernels
.5 ounces shallots, finely diced
1 ounce cream
.5 ounces butter
.25 ounces chopped garlic

Sauté garlic, shallots and corn. Add cream, then tomato. Mount in the butter at the end.

Crab Cake Preparation:

3 ounces jumbo lump crabmeat
.5 ounces red onion, finely diced
.5 ounces red and green pepper, finely diced
.25 ounces fresh thyme, chopped
.5 ounces mayonnaise
4 ounces crab cake mix
Salt and black pepper to taste

Preheat oven to 250 degrees.
Stir crabmeat together with onions, peppers, thyme and mayonnaise.
Add crab cake mix and stir until thoroughly incorporated.
Season mixture to taste with salt and black pepper.
Form mixture into a cake.
Place a 4 ounce stainless steel ring into an ovenproof skillet and heat the skillet over a medium high flame.
Slip the Crab Cake into the stainless steel ring and sear on both sides, turning once.
Transfer skillet to preheated oven and bake Crab Cake for 2 minutes.

Garnish:

.5 ounces micro-greens

To serve:

Drizzle the Moque Choux on top of the Crab Cake and garnish with micro-greens.

Seafood Etouffée

Yield: 4 servings

4 ounces onion
4 ounces celery
4 ounces green peppers
2 ounces garlic
8 medium tomatoes, seeded and diced
2 ounces Brown Roux (see below)
12 head-on, peeled shrimp
8 ounces oysters
8 ounces redfish, in chunks
6 ounces crabmeat
2 ounces thyme
1 gallon fish stock
Cayenne pepper
Creole seasoning
Cooked rice (6 ounces dry)
1 baguette

Brown Roux:

¾ cup oil (canola or vegetable)
1 cup all-purpose white flour

Heat a heavy skillet or cast iron pot and add ¾ cup oil. When oil is hot, add flour slowly, stirring constantly. Cook over medium heat, continuing to stir, until flour and oil blend, thicken and brown.

Seafood Etouffée:

In a large pot, sauté garlic, onions, celery and green peppers.
Season to taste with cayenne pepper and Creole seasoning; add thyme.
Add fish stock and bring to boil.
Whisk in Brown Roux.
Stir in tomatoes and cook for 3 minutes.
Fold in gently the shrimp, oysters, fish and crabmeat, taking care not to break up pieces of seafood.
Simmer gently, removing from heat as soon as shrimp and oysters are cooked.
Serve over rice with slices of baguette.

Mélange

Looking for alligator? Mulate's makes a mean Grilled or Fried Alligator Po-Boy. This 'gator po-boy goes great with a cup of Zydeco Gumbo to make a satisfying, authentic Cajun lunch. The menu boasts Fried or Sautéed Crab Claws, Fried Catfish, Shrimp and Oysters en Brochette and Mulate's Cajun Boudin, along with other delectable specialties one would hope to find at "The Original Cajun Restaurant." The first Mulate's, founded by restaurateur Kerry Boutté, continues to operate in Breaux Bridge, Louisiana. A second Mulate's serves lucky diners in Baton Rouge. The third and newest Mulate's caters to enthusiastic patrons in the French Quarter. Monique Boutté Christina, daughter of founder Kerry Boutté, runs the French Quarter restaurant. Cajuns of all ages and non-Cajuns, as well, flock to this lively restaurant and dance hall to kick up their heels and let the good times roll. Open 7 days a week, lunch and dinner. Live Cajun bands with dancing nightly. Mulate's is open and hopping every day. *Laissez les bons temps rouler!*

Chicken and Sausage Jambalaya

Yield: 8 servings

2 tablespoons Mulate's Cajun Seasoning
1 pound boneless, skinless chicken thighs
1 pound boneless, skinless chicken breasts
1 tablespoon oil
2 sticks margarine
2 cups water
4 medium onions, diced
1 medium bell pepper, diced
3 cloves garlic, chopped
1 pound smoked sausage, cut into ½ inch pieces
1 pint fresh mushrooms, sliced
1 can (10 ounce) RO*TEL Diced Tomatoes and Green Chilies
4 cups cooked rice

Season all chicken pieces.
In a large pot, heat oil and brown chicken.
Remove chicken from pot and cut into bite-sized pieces.
Add margarine, ½ cup water and onions to pot.
Cook onions over medium high heat about 30-40 minutes, or until dark golden brown; add water as needed to prevent sticking.
Add bell pepper and garlic. Continue to cook, stirring frequently, 15 minutes more.
Add chicken, sausage, RO*TEL and any remaining water to pot.
Reduce heat to medium low and cook for 45 minutes, stirring occasionally.
Mix with cooked rice.

Crawfish Etouffée

Yield: 4 servings

½ stick butter
1 medium onion, diced
1 small bell pepper, diced
1 teaspoon salt
1 teaspoon cayenne pepper
2 teaspoons flour
½ cup water
1 pound peeled crawfish tails
¼ cup chopped green onions
2 cups cooked white rice

In a large saucepan, melt butter over medium heat.
Add onion and bell pepper; cook until transparent and tender, about 15 minutes. Add seasonings, then flour, stirring constantly.
Add water; mix well. Add crawfish and simmer for 10 minutes. Add green onions and simmer for 3 minutes.
Serve over rice.

Fried Crawfish

Yield: 4-6 servings

2 pounds peeled crawfish tails
3 cups flour
2-3 teaspoons salt
1 teaspoon cayenne pepper
1 cup milk
2 eggs, beaten
2-3 cups oil for frying

Rinse and dry crawfish. Place flour in a 9"x 13" pan. Add salt and cayenne pepper to your taste; mix well. In a shallow bowl, mix milk and eggs. Dip crawfish into egg wash, then toss in flour mixture, to coat well. Fry in oil at 375 degrees for 4-5 minutes. Serve with cocktail sauce.

Mulate's

201 Julia St. • New Orleans 70130 • Tel 504-522-1492

THE NEW ORLEANS GRILL
at Windsor Court Hotel

The NewOrleans Grill Room appears on "best of" lists all around: Zagat's Top Ten Restaurants, *Condé Nast Traveler*'s Top 100 Best in World for 2002 and 2003, and *Food and Wine*'s Top 50 Best Hotel Restaurants in America. The kitchen of Chef Brett Breaux and Chef Greg Sonnier serves breakfast, lunch and dinner seven days a week. The menu of New American cuisine challenges even foodies--- I studied the mouth-watering items on the menu in frustration, wanting to try them all. At dinner, while no one was looking, I dipped my hot-from-the-oven bread into the killer dressing on The Classic Windsor Court Salad of eggs, bacon, avocado, tomatoes, radishes... Mmmmmmmm…..... Artfully prepared food presented in an artful manner. Spectacular, original murals, soft lighting, classical music in the background, large bouquets of fresh flowers. At The New Orleans Grill Room, diners receive the royal treatment without a hint of intimidation.

Sea Scallops with Roasted Red Pepper Sauce

Yield: 2 servings

2 red bell peppers
1 tablespoon butter
½ teaspoon minced garlic
2 cups heavy cream
½ teaspoon salt
Olive oil
Creole seasoning to taste
8 sea scallops
1 ounce fresh chopped chives

Method:

Roast peppers in 400 degree oven until very dark. Place roasted peppers in a paper bag and close the bag. Let peppers rest for 15 minutes. Peel peppers, removing seeds and ribs. Purée in blender or food processor until very smooth. Add pepper purée, butter and garlic to a medium saucepan. Cook to reduce sauce for 3 minutes. Add salt and pepper. Set aside and keep warm.

Lightly season scallops with Creole seasoning. Add olive oil to a saucepan and heat over medium high heat. Place seasoned scallops in pan and sear on both sides until lightly browned. Allow 4-6 minutes for searing. Scallops should be medium hot in center when searing is completed. (If scallops do not reach medium hot in center after 4-6 minutes of searing, finish cooking them in a hot oven.)

To Serve:

Place cooked scallops on a warm serving dish. Pour roasted red pepper sauce over scallops and garnish with fresh chopped chives.

The New Orleans Grill Room

300 Gravier St. • New Orleans 70130 • Tel 888-596-0955

Don't miss this old-line, uptown eating establishment serving classic Italian and Creole cuisine since 1913. Before or after a Saints' game or any other occasion, nothing beats the camaraderie in the oyster bar, where one waits happily for a table in the dining room. Pascal's Manale, home of the Original B-B-Q Shrimp, is famous for this particular dish. Like other New Orleans restaurants, Pascal's Manale has had its fair share of celebrity patrons: Cyndi Lauper, Bear Bryant, Ernest Borgnine and Merv Griffin. Overshadowed possibly by the famous Original B-B-Q Shrimp, the Bread Pudding has received less press than I think it deserves. By my lights, and I consider myself a true connoisseur of bread pudding, Manale's Bread Pudding is one of the best in N'awlins.

Frutta Del Mare

Yield: 1 large serving or 2 small servings

3 ounces olive oil
10 15-count scallops
3-4 raw oysters
3 large peeled and deveined shrimp
2 ounces jumbo lump crabmeat
¼ teaspoon each: black pepper, white pepper and salt
8 ounces seafood stock
6 ounces marinara sauce
1 teaspoon chopped fresh garlic
½ cup chopped green onions
½ teaspoon crushed red pepper
2 ounces brandy
8 ounces cooked pasta
1 ounce white wine
Chopped parsley for garnish

Over medium high flame, heat skillet and then add olive oil.
Next, add scallops and cook briefly until scallops start to brown.
Add shrimp along with crushed red pepper and salt to taste.
Add garlic and continue to cook until garlic just begins to brown.
Add green onions.
Add brandy, stand back from pan and set brandy aflame.
As soon as flame dies down, add marinara sauce and cook 2 minutes.
Add pasta and white wine to pan.
Continue cooking briefly, until liquid is reduced by half.

To Plate:
Arrange serving of pasta on plate, then ladle seafood with sauce onto pasta. Garnish with chopped parsley.

Prosciutto Peppers and Shrimp

Yield: 1 large serving or 2 small servings

2 ounces thinly sliced prosciutto ham
7 peeled and deveined 21-25 count shrimp
1 ounce roasted red pepper
1 teaspoon chopped garlic
1 ounce chopped green onion
1 teaspoon chopped parsley
2 ounces feta cheese
2 ounces butter
4 ounces shrimp stock
2 ounces vodka
Salt, pepper and crushed red pepper to taste
8 ounces cooked bowtie pasta

In medium sauté pan heat olive oil. Add prosciutto ham and cook until crisp.
Add shrimp and cook briefly (until about halfway done).
Add vodka to pan, stand back and set vodka aflame to deglaze pan.
After flame dies down, add peppers, garlic, green onion, parsley and feta cheese.
Cook for 2-3 minutes.
Add butter and stock, bring to simmer and reduce for 3-4 minutes.
Add salt and pepper.
Add bowtie pasta and cook just until pasta is heated through.

To Plate:
Serve in a pasta bowl, garnished with parsley.

1838 Napoleon Ave. • New Orleans 70115 •Tel 504-895-4877

Like many New Orleans chefs, Thomas Wolfe has been showered with honors. Chef Wolfe's ability to focus is remarkable: He oversees not just one, but two dining establishments where excellence is the order of every day. At Peristyle, I relished Chef Wolfe's Roasted Gulf Shrimp and Creole Risotto, set in Tomato Cream. I had to pass up the Steamed Mussels and Cockle Clams, with celeriac and saffron aioli. After all, how many entrées can a single diner devour, with decorum, at one sitting? For dessert, the Vanilla Cheesecake was fluffy, light, not too sweet, with warm raspberry sauce, whipped cream and fresh mint leaves. Best ever! Puts old fashioned cheesecake with strawberries to shame. At Wolfe's in the Warehouse, the signature dish is Duck Duck Goose. Deadly delicious. Peristyle serves dinner Tuesdays through Saturdays; lunch on Fridays.

Chorizo Sausage Congris

Yield: 5 servings

Chorizo Sausage and Rice
½ pound chorizo sausage
1 small yellow onion, diced
1 tablespoon chopped garlic
2 tablespoons sliced green onions
2 ¼ cups steamed rice

Render chorizo sausage until browned.
Add onions, garlic and green onions.
Cook until yellow onions are translucent.
Add steamed rice and sauté 3-4 minutes.

Cilantro Black Bean Purée
1 pound dry black beans
¾ pound medium sized onions
1 tablespoon chopped garlic
1 ½ bay leaves
2 ribs celery, diced
½ cup concasse (tomatoes: blanched, peeled, seeded, chopped to ¼" dice)
½ green bell pepper, diced
1 jalapeño, minced
½ teaspoon ground black pepper
1 cup fresh cilantro
1 cup crab stock
¾ teaspoon ground coriander
½ teaspoon ground cumin
1 teaspoon salt; additional salt to taste.

Soak beans in a generous amount of water overnight.
Drain beans.
In a large pot, sauté onions, garlic, celery, concasse and bell pepper.
Add beans and all remaining ingredients.
Add water to bring liquid to depth of about 1" above beans and vegetables.
Simmer beans until they are very tender.
Remove from pot ¼ of cooked beans and set aside. Purée the remaining ¾ of the beans.
Fold the whole beans back into the purée. Season with salt to taste.

Set:
1 ¼ tablespoon chopped fresh cilantro
¾ cup diced fresh tomatoes
Salt and black pepper

To Assemble Congris:
Fold 2 cups of Cilantro Black Bean Purée,
1 ¼ tablespoons chopped fresh cilantro and
¾ cup diced fresh tomatoes into
the Chorizo Sausage and Rice.
Season with salt and
pepper to taste.

1041 Dumaine St. • New Orleans 70116 • Tel 504-593-9535

At Victoria Inn and Gardens in Lafitte, guests can kick back and relax while Roy and Dale Ross, the perfect hosts, see to the details. Guest dine *well*. Crabmeat Omelette with Fresh Fruit for breakfast: the best! From Chef Matt Regan's dinner menu, I chose Seafood Filled Artichoke with Bearnaise Sauce, Bacon Wrapped Shrimp and Baked Oysters. Beautiful gardens, private dock, swimming pool. After a few days of rural paradise, I returned to N'awlins and checked in at The House on Bayou Road, a 2-acre urban retreat near the Quarter. Breakfast at this "Petite Creole Plantation" included fresh figs grown on the premises. Recommended in *1,000 Places in the U.S.A. and Canada to See Before You Die* (Workman Publishing, May 2007). Experience both these B & Bs for the best of Cajun country and Creole luxury.

Seafood Gumbo

Yield: 8-10 servings

Seafood for Gumbo:
2 pounds shrimp (headed and peeled, save heads)
1 quart oysters (unwashed, with oyster liquor)
1 quart crab claws

Ingredients for Stock:
3 quarts water
Shrimp heads (saved from 2 pounds shrimp, see above)
1 pound gumbo crabs

Ingredients for Roux:
2 tablespoons oil
2 tablespoons flour

Ingredients for Vegetable Mixture:
2 tablespoons oil
3 cups sliced okra
1 large chopped onion
1 16-ounce can peeled, chopped tomatoes
1 bay leaf
1 teaspoon salt
3 cloves garlic, peeled and minced
½ teaspoon cayenne pepper
8-10 servings cooked rice

Prepare a dark roux with 2 tablespoons oil and 2 tablespoons flour; set aside. Prepare seafood stock with shrimp heads, gumbo crabs and 3 quarts water. Strain stock to remove solids; discard solids. Separate oysters from oyster liquor. Set oysters aside. Add the oyster liquor to the strained seafood stock. Set aside in reserve. In a large pot, smother okra and onions in oil. Stir often to avoid burning onions. When okra is almost cooked, add tomatoes and cook for another 15 minutes. Add bay leaf, garlic, salt and pepper and cook for 10 minutes more. Add roux to vegetable mixture. Stirring as you pour, slowly add reserved stock to vegetable mixture. Add shrimp, oysters and crab claws. Cook for 30 minutes. Serve gumbo over rice.

Lemon Meringue Pie

¾ cup sugar
2 tablespoons flour
2 tablespoons cornstarch
¼ teaspoon salt
1 ¼ cups hot water
2 lemons
2 eggs at room temperature, separated
1 tablespoon butter
1 baked pie shell

Filling:
Use a lemon zester or a fine grater to remove thin yellow portion of rind from both lemons. (Because white portion of rind is bitter, use ONLY the yellow layer.) Each lemon should yield about 1 teaspoon of grated yellow rind. Set aside grated lemon rind. Squeeze juice from whole lemons and reserve. Mix sugar, flour, cornstarch and salt in saucepan. Add hot water. Cook over medium heat, stirring until mixture thickens. Add reserved lemon juice and lemon rind to mixture in saucepan. Add egg yolks and cook until mixture starts to bubble. Remove filling from heat. Add butter. Pour filling into baked pie shell.

Meringue:
Cooking Tips: *Use containers and equipment free of all traces of oil. Allow the egg whites to reach room temperature (about 75 degrees) before you begin work.*

Place room temperature egg whites in clean bowl. Whip at high speed with electric mixer. When soft peaks form, slowly add ¼ cup sugar. Continue beating just until stiff peaks form; do not overbeat. Top pie with meringue. Brown the meringue by placing the pie very briefly under a hot broiler. Meringue burns quickly---BE CAREFUL!

The Restaurant at Victoria Inn

4707 Jean Lafitte Blvd. • Lafitte 70067 • Tel 1-800-689-4797

Talented Chef Bob Iacovone came to Cuvée with a very impressive culinary background and has been with the restaurant since its pre-opening period in 1999. "Contemporary Creole-Continental" is Cuvée's style. Menu notes are a tip-off that Cuvée's cuisine is other than traditional. Case in point: "Spaghetti and Meatball" in Chef Iacovone's language is a large scallop with caper berries and tomato brunoise over spaghetti squash. Scrumptious. Cuvée's name suggests an emphasis on wine. Indeed, Chef Iacovone's credentials include a first-level certificate from The Court of Sommeliers in London: Cuvée's cellar is stocked with 650 select wines from the Americas, Europe and Australia. Cuvée is posh, certainly, but this is a warm and delightful New Orleans kind of posh. Cuvée is a recent winner in *2007 Best of New Orleans Restaurant Guide,* produced by Zagat for Top Creole.

Coq Au Vin Blanc

Yield: 5 servings

2 pounds chicken thigh meat, trimmed of excess fat
1 cup olive oil
1 carrot, peeled and diced
1 stalk celery, diced
1 white onion, diced
4 cloves garlic, chopped
¾ cup all purpose flour
1 bottle white wine
1 cup Madeira wine
1 cup sherry vinegar
½ gallon chicken stock
1 bunch fresh thyme, chopped
1 bunch flat leaf parsley, chopped
Salt and pepper to taste

Method:

In a large pot, heat oil on medium heat.
Add chicken thighs and cook until done, turning thighs once. Remove thighs from oil and set aside. Add onions, celery, carrots and garlic to oil. Stirring often, cook until slightly browned. Add flour to vegetable mixture and stir constantly 5 minutes to make a roux. Add white wine, Madeira wine and sherry vinegar to roux and boil for 5 minutes, stirring often.
Add chicken stock and bring to boil.
Reduce heat and simmer mixture until it reaches consistency of gravy.
Add fresh herbs; place chicken thighs in sauce. Serve over rice or mashed potatoes.

Mustard and Herb Crusted Salmon with Crab and Brie Orzo and Lemon Confit

Yield: 4 servings

Mustard and Herb Crusted Salmon:
4 7-ounce salmon fillets
½ cup vegetable or olive oil
½ cup flour
½ cup dry mustard
½ cup grated Parmesan
1 tablespoon finely chopped fresh basil
1 tablespoon finely chopped fresh thyme
1 tablespoon finely chopped fresh parsley

Crab and Brie Orzo:
2 cups orzo
½ gallon salted boiling water
1 pint heavy cream
4 ounces Brie cheese, cut into large pieces
Salt and pepper
½ pound crabmeat, lump or backfin, picked thoroughly for shells

Lemon Confit:
1 lemon, seeded and thinly sliced
1 gallon water
2 cups champagne vinegar
1 cup sugar

Preparation:
Combine flour, dry mustard and grated Parmesan. Combine fresh chopped herbs. Cook orzo in boiling water until *al dente*. Combine lemon slices with water, vinegar and sugar. Bring to a rapid simmer and cook until lemon slices are tender. Remove lemon slices from water and let cool. Scald the heavy cream and remove from heat at once. Add Brie cheese, salt and pepper and stir to a creamy consistency. In a large sauté pan, combine the Brie cream mixture with the cooked orzo. Stir over medium flame until mixture is hot. Add crabmeat to the pan with Brie and orzo; stir until combined. Remove pan from heat and set aside. Coat the salmon fillets with salt, pepper and fresh herbs. Place fillets in the mustard mix and turn to coat both sides. Heat oil in large sauté pan and sauté fillets on both sides, cooking until they are golden brown.

To Plate:
Arrange a portion of Crab and Brie Orzo in center of plate. Top with a salmon fillet. Top the fillet with a slice of Lemon Confit.

Restaurant Cuvée

322 Magazine Street • New Orleans 70130 • Tel 504-587-9001

"Mirror, mirror on the wall, who is the fairest of them all?" At Riche, with mirrors everywhere and marvelous fare, you, too, might come to feel a little vain and spoiled. Contemporary décor complements perfectly the contemporary French brasserie cuisine. Grilled Hanger Steak and Arugula Citrus Salad are among the lunch menu offerings. Among the dinner entrées, consider Duck Confit or Redfish Meunière, Rock Shrimp and Espelette Pepper. If something grand is what you're looking for, try the Bouillabaisse: lobster, clams, mussels, shrimp, scallops and rouille. No skimping on desserts at Riche, please. I chose the Vanilla Bean Soufflé. Sensational. A *Bon Appétit* "Restaurateur of the Year," Chef Todd English has also been honored by the James Beard Foundation. Riche is located in Harrah's Hotel, which is just by the French Quarter. Open 7 days a week for lunch and dinner.

Frisée Aux Lardons

Yield: 4 servings

12 ounces frisée (yellow and tender)
1 ounce chives, minced
8 ounces bacon Lardons (recipe below)
6 ounces Lemon Vinaigrette (recipe below)
1 ounce kosher salt
4 turns of pepper mill, fresh whole black pepper
4 soft poached eggs
Gruyère Croutons (recipe below)

Lemon Vinaigrette:
3 ounces fresh squeezed lemon juice
6 ounces extra virgin olive oil
1 tablespoon Dijon mustard
1 teaspoon kosher salt
1 turn of pepper mill, fresh whole black pepper

In a salad bowl whisk together lemon juice, Dijon mustard and seasonings.
Whisking constantly, slowly drizzle in extra virgin olive oil and continue to whisk until dressing emulsifies.

Gruyère Croutons:
1 fresh baguette, split lengthwise
2 tablespoons extra virgin olive oil
4 ounces Gruyère cheese, shredded
1 tablespoon kosher salt
3 turns of pepper mill, fresh whole black pepper

Season baguette halves with extra virgin olive oil, salt and pepper; place shredded Gruyère on top. Toast bread until it is light brown and crispy. Let cool to room temperature. Cut each baguette half into 6 pieces to make large 12 croutons.

Lardons:
Cut raw bacon slab into ½-inch cubes.
Poach bacon cubes in water for 10 minutes, or until soft; let drain.
Sauté bacon until brown and crisp; remove Lardons from grease and set aside on paper towels to cool slightly and to drain.

To Prepare Salad:
Wash and dry frisée; tear into pieces.
Add frisée, along with 1 ounce kosher salt and 4 turns pepper, to salad bowl with Lemon Vinaigrette; toss together.

To Serve:
Pile equal portions of dressed salad onto 4 individual serving plates.
Top each serving with a poached egg.
Arrange 3 croutons on each plate, for dipping in the poached eggs.

Riche by Todd English

228 Poydras St. • New Orleans 70130 • Tel 504-533-6117

Located at the Wyndham Riverfront Hotel, 7 on Fulton offers contemporary Louisiana cuisine that will please the most discriminating palate. Chef Michael Sichel, an enthusiastic and engaging fellow, obviously appreciates his customers and recognizes that everyone brings something to the table, so to speak. Menu items change often and have included Foie Gras Torchon, White Bean Vichyssoise, Caramelized Scallops, Seared Tuna and Beef Strip Loin au Poivre. Foodies who "want it all" may call a day in advance and order The Chef's Selection---a generous sampling of Chef Sichel's own current favorites. Sophisticated atmosphere; friendly staff. Live music every Thursday night. Open for all meals. Children's menu offered.

Chilled Creole Tomato Soup

Yield: 4 servings

Soup:
3 pounds Creole tomatoes (very ripe tomatoes may be used)
1 jalapeño pepper
1 stem basil
Pinch of salt

Garnish:
16 Louisiana shrimp
1 cup olive oil
2 jalapeño peppers
2 tablespoons red wine vinegar
1 stem basil

Directions for Soup:
Cut all tomatoes into quarters. Cut jalapeño pepper in half. Place tomatoes, jalapeño, the basil stem and a pinch of salt in a pot with 2 cups water. Bring to a simmer; continue to simmer for 1½ hours. The natural juices of the tomatoes will release—that intense flavor is your broth. Strain the soup through a fine strainer or cheesecloth to remove any sediment. Refrigerate soup until cold.

Directions for Garnish:
Clean and devein shrimp. Grill quickly to medium rare. Place grilled shrimp in a bowl with olive oil, red vinegar, a basil stem and the juice of 1 jalapeño. This marinade will continue to cook the shrimp and will infuse the shrimp with flavors. Cover bowl and refrigerate. Cut 1 jalapeño pepper into slivers and reserve.

To Serve:
Pour tomato broth equally into 4 chilled bowls. Remove shrimp from marinade; blot off excess marinade with paper towels. Place 4 shrimp in each bowl and garnish with reserved jalapeño slivers.

Chef's Comment: *"cool, refreshing and Louisiana"*

Nine-Minute Cookies and Iced Milk

Yield: 30 cookies

4 ounces brown sugar
4 ounces granulated sugar
4 ounces softened butter
1 egg
1 teaspoon vanilla extract
4 ounces cake flour
4 ounces all-purpose flour
Pinch of salt
8 ounces chocolate chips

Cold milk, served from frozen glasses

Directions:
In mixer with paddle attachment, mix sugars, butter, egg and vanilla together until creamy.
Sift flour and place into a large bowl with chocolate chips. Add creamy mixture to bowl with flour and chips and fold together.
Roll dough into a log and refrigerate.

When log of dough is cool, slice into medallions ½ inch thick.
Place medallions on a sheet pan and bake in preheated 375 degree oven for 7 minutes.

Serving:
Allow cookies to cool for 1 minute. Serve warm, with cold, cold milk.

Chef's Comment: *"childhood memories"*

701 Fulton Street • New Orleans 70130 • Tel 504-525-7555

New Orleans Magazine readers named Chef Scott Boswell, owner of Stella!, Best Chef 2006. A Louisiana native and a graduate of the Culinary Institute of America, Chef Boswell brings a world of culinary experience (he's worked in Tokyo, Kobe, Provence, Florence) to his innovative, classically executed dishes. Global-Modern cuisine: French, Italian, Asian and Creole cooking influences result in "food that shouts with a uniquely global voice" (www.restaurantstella.com). Menu changes daily, but here's a sampler: Crisp Veal and Kobayaki Gyoza Dumplings with Tempura Shiso Leaves and Two Spicy Peanut Sauces; Caramelized Wild Burgundy Escargots with Fresh Thyme, Local Garlic, Lemon Zest, Basil Pistou and Lavender Meringue; Almond and Herb Crusted Rack of Australian Lamb. Open nightly. You'll find Stella! next to the historic Hotel Provincial, with valet parking for Stella! diners. For a casual New Orleans breakfast or lunch, try Stella!'s sister restaurant, Stanley!, serving American cuisine around the corner on Jackson Square.

Bananas Foster French Toast with Crispy Plantains and Spicy Candied Walnuts

Yield: 4 servings

Spicy Candied Walnuts:
1 cup walnuts, toasted
1 cup confectioner's sugar
1 tablespoon cinnamon
¼ teaspoon cayenne pepper
3 tablespoons granulated sugar
1 quart boiling water
1 quart peanut oil, for frying
¼ teaspoon nutmeg

Crispy Plantains:
1 green plantain
1 quart peanut oil (same as used to cook Spicy Candied Walnuts)

French Toast:
2 eggs
1 French baguette or other French style bread, sliced

½ cup (1 stick) unsalted butter
¼ teaspoon nutmeg
1 cup half-and-half
1 teaspoon cinnamon
1 tablespoon granulated sugar

Bananas Foster Sauce:
½ pound (2 sticks) unsalted butter
2 teaspoons cinnamon
½ ounce banana liqueur
2 bananas, peeled and sliced into thin sticks
Confectioner's sugar for dusting
2 cups light brown sugar
½ teaspoon nutmeg
2 ounces light rum

For topping and garnish:
1 quart vanilla bean ice cream
4 mint sprigs

To make Spicy Candied Walnuts:
Place a wire rack on a baking sheet. Place the toasted nuts in a handheld strainer and submerse in boiling water for 30 seconds. Remove and blot dry on a towel. Toss in a bowl with confectioner's sugar. Heat peanut oil in deep fryer or deep saucepan until almost smoking. Working with half the nuts at a time, put the nuts back into the strainer and lower into the hot oil for 5 seconds. Remove nuts from oil and transfer to wire rack. Mix cinnamon, nutmeg, cayenne, sugar and salt together and dust over the hot walnuts. Allow to cool. Set heated peanut oil aside.

To prepare Crispy Plantains:
Peel the plantain and slice lengthwise into thin strips on a mandoline or a V-slicer. Reheat the peanut oil to

370 degrees. Drop plantain slices into hot oil and fry until they become crisp and float to the top. Remove plantains with slotted spoon or wire skimmer and drain on paper towels. Set aside until ready to use.

To prepare French Toast:
Place wire rack on baking sheet. In a shallow bowl, mix eggs and half-and-half, whisking slightly to break up the eggs. Soak bread slices in egg mixture. Melt butter in large nonstick sauté pan or skillet over medium high heat. Sauté soaked bread slices in butter until deep golden brown on both sides. Lift with tongs and place on wire rack. Mix cinnamon, nutmeg and sugar; dust over bread slices. Set aside and keep warm.

To prepare Bananas Foster Sauce:
Melt butter, brown sugar, cinnamon and nutmeg in small sauté pan or skillet over medium heat. When bubbling hot, add liqueur and rum. Avert your face and ignite mixture with a match. Shake the pan until the alcohol burns off and the flame dies down. Add banana slices and toss until coated. Set aside and keep warm.

To plate:
Serve one tablespoon Bananas Foster Sauce in center of each plate. Lay two pieces of French Toast on top of sauce. Form quenelles of ice cream and place one on each piece of French Toast. Spoon Bananas Foster Sauce over ice cream quenelles and French Toast. Dust the Crispy Plantains with confectioner's sugar and stand them in the ice cream quenelles. Garnish with Spicy Candied Walnuts and a sprig of mint.

Stella!

1032 Chartres St. • New Orleans 70116 • Tel 504-587-0091

This historic Garden District B & B offers visitors a glimpse of the 1890's, when the mansion was built as a private home. Owners Guy and Nancy Fournier serve serious New Orleans breakfasts. Great French toast! Those visiting around Passover might have the good fortune to try Matzo Brie, a Jewish tradition for some. For lunch and dinner, guests have great options. Nearby: Commander's Palace, Upperline, Felix's Uptown and La Crêpe Nanou. Also convenient: Lilette's, known for fine French-Italian cuisine and for the Pork Belly Sandwich. This sandwich, the all-time favorite of a good friend, spells comfort. Chow down and bliss out! Lilette's also serves "Sizzlingly Shrimp," in a little cast iron skillet — simple and spicy. Perfectly located B & B for visitors in search of a true N'awlins experience.

Creole Bread Pudding

Yield: 8 servings

½ pound Linguisa sausage, chopped, casings removed
½ cup minced onions
¼ cup chopped green peppers
1/3 cup sliced green onions
½ cup dry white wine
¼ cup melted butter
8 cups day old French bread, cut into 1" cubes
2 ½ cups milk
½ cup heavy cream
8 eggs
½ pound pepper jack cheese, grated
½ pound Monterey jack cheese, grated
¾ teaspoon salt
1/8 teaspoon cayenne
¾ cup sour cream
½ cup Parmesan cheese, grated

Heat oven to 325 degrees.
Heat sauté pan and cook sausage until golden.
Add onions, bell peppers and green onions; cook until softened.
Add wine and reduce heat slightly, continuing to cook and stir for 1 minute.
Remove from heat.
Place bread in large bowl.
In another bowl, beat eggs and mix with milk and cream. Pour this mixture over bread in large bowl and allow to sit 5 minutes.
Coat 10" x 13" casserole dish evenly with melted butter.

Pour extra melted butter over bread.
Add sausage mixture, pepper jack and Monterey jack cheeses and spices to large bowl with bread and fold all ingredients together. Cover with foil and bake 15 minutes. Remove casserole from oven and increase temperature to 375 degrees.
Remove foil from casserole. Spoon sour cream evenly over bread pudding and top with Parmesan cheese. Return casserole to oven and bake 15-20 minutes longer. Serve hot.

French Toast

Yield: 8 servings

Toast:
16 slices dense French bread, ¾" thick
8 eggs
2 cups milk
½ cup sugar
¼ cup orange juice
1 teaspoon nutmeg
1 teaspoon vanilla extract
1 teaspoon salt
2/3 cup butter

Topping:
1 cup coarsely chopped pecans
½ cup tightly packed brown sugar
2 tablespoons melted butter

Prepare Toast: Arrange bread slices in single layer in baking dish. In a bowl, whisk together eggs, milk, orange juice, sugar, nutmeg, salt and vanilla until blended and frothy. Pour mixture evenly over bread and refrigerate, covered, overnight.
In 400 degree oven, melt 2/3 cup butter in 10" x 15" baking pan. Tilt pan to coat sides with butter. Arrange saturated bread in single layer in buttered baking pan. Pour excess egg mixture over the bread slices. With oven still at 400 degrees, bake bread 25 minutes, until light brown and firm.

Prepare Topping: Mix pecans, brown sugar and melted butter.

To Serve: Sprinkle topping over toast. Broil for 4 minutes, about 5 inches from the heat. Serve immediately.

Sully Mansion Bed and Breakfast

2631 Prytania Street • New Orleans 70130 • Tel 504-891-0457

Tujague's has been serving diners in the French Quarter for 150+ years now. This neighborhood classic holds special status as New Orleans' second oldest restaurant. Enjoy the traditional House Specialty, Beef Brisket with Creole Sauce, or on the other hand, you might try the mouth-watering Garlic Chicken, which is not actually on the menu. In terms of presentation, I'd say the Garlic Chicken was a sight for sore eyes. Plus, it tasted every bit as good as it looked. To arrange for your Garlic Chicken Experience, definitely call in advance---a few hours' notice, same day, is generally sufficient. Lunch: 11 a.m. to 3 p.m.; Dinner: 5 p.m. to 11:00 p.m.

Crab and Spinach Bisque

Yield: 10-12 servings

4 10-ounce bags fresh spinach
1 pound butter
3/8 cup flour
¾ cup cream cheese
1 cup milk
2 pints whipping cream
1 pound crabmeat
½ can chicken stock or 1 can chicken bouillon
Pinch of white pepper

Chop spinach fine. If using a food processor,
do not purée. Set aside with its juice. Melt butter in a
large pot. Add flour and stir until smooth, making sure
no lumps remain. Add cream, crabmeat and chicken
broth or bouillon. Add spinach and simmer.
In a separate saucepan over a low flame, heat cream
cheese until completely melted and smooth. Add milk
to cream cheese and stir. Add cream cheese mixture to
soup in large pot. Season with white pepper.
Cook for 5 minutes. Soup will be thick. To thin, slowly
add water until bisque reaches desired consistency.

Remoulade Sauce

Yield: about two quarts

3 cups finely chopped white onion
1 cup finely chopped celery
1 cup finely chopped green onions
1 cup finely chopped fresh parsley
1 cup finely chopped lettuce
16 ounces Creole mustard or brown mustard
1 ½ pints olive oil
¼ cup fresh lemon juice
Generous amount of paprika, for color

Mix all chopped vegetables together. Add Creole
mustard and mix well. Add paprika, olive oil and salt
and pepper to taste. Sauce can be made in advance and
will keep refrigerated for several days.

Tujague's

823 Decatur St • New Orleans 70116 • Tel 504-525-8676

P roprietor/General Manager JoAnn Clevenger and Executive Chef Kevin Smith believe strongly in art on the walls and art on the plates. One writer pointed out that although the museums close early, visitors to New Orleans can continue to view regional art after hours, while dining at the Upperline. JoAnn Clevenger sets the scene as the spirited and art-loving hostess. Chef Smith focuses on the cuisine, which continues to draw national attention. You MUST try the The Original Fried Green Tomato with Shrimp Remoulade. Fitting accompaniments? Veal Grillades with Cheddar Grits, Lamb Shank Braised in Wine, Cane River Country Shrimp, Duck and Andouille Gumbo or Spicy Crispy Oysters St. Claude. If you really want to push the envelope, try the Drum Piquant with Hot and Hot Shrimp, one of *USA Today's* "Top 25 Dishes for 2006." Open nightly Wednesday through Sunday. Reservations strongly recommended.

The Original Fried Green Tomato with Shrimp Remoulade

Yield: 4 servings as appetizer

In 1992, JoAnn Clevenger of Upperline Restaurant created this combination of two traditional Louisiana favorites. No one copied it until about 1995. Since then it has appeared on menus all over the USA (Seattle, Chicago, Charleston, etc.) and has become part of the New Orleans repertoire. Local chefs and home cooks have created their own versions. Here is the Upperline recipe from Chef Ken Smith.

Fried Green Tomatoes:

1 cup buttermilk
8 slices green tomatoes (completely green, if possible), about ½" thick
1 cup corn flour, lightly seasoned with salt and black or white pepper
4-6 tablespoons vegetable oil
Handful of mixed greens for garnish
24 medium shrimp, poached, peeled and chilled
1 cup (approximately) chilled remoulade sauce, homemade or purchased (see Chef's Notes)

Pour buttermilk into a medium bowl; put seasoned corn flour into a shallow dish.
Begin to heat oil in a large sauté pan over moderate heat.

While oil heats, dip tomato slices into milk, then coat with corn flour.
Place tomato slices into sauté pan in a single layer. Do not crowd. Cook tomato slices over moderate heat until golden brown on bottom; turn slices and allow to brown on the other side. Allow total cooking time of about 3-4 minutes. When done, the tomatoes should be golden brown and cooked through, but not mushy.

To Serve:

Serve tomatoes warm or hot. Shrimp and remoulade sauce should be cold.
On each plate, arrange 2 tomato slices next to each other. Top each slice with 3 chilled shrimp. Spoon 1½ tablespoons remoulade sauce over the shrimp on each slice. Garnish plate with a few mixed greens.

Chef's Notes: *Crawfish, scallops or lobster may be substituted successfully for shrimp in this recipe. Alternatively, eliminate the shrimp and serve remoulade sauce directly on the tomato slices for an appetizer that is quite tasty and a bit simpler. To simplify even further, you might use Arnaud's brand of remoulade sauce. Arnaud's brand is available at specialty shops and on the web (www.arnaudsstore.com).*

Syrup Cake (Gateau De Sirop)

½ vegetable oil
1 ½ cup Steen's 100% Pure Cane Syrup
1 egg, beaten
2 ½ cups sifted all-purpose flour
1 teaspoon cinnamon
1 teaspoon ginger
½ teaspoon salt
1 ½ teaspoons baking soda
¾ cup hot water
Powdered sugar

Preheat oven to 350 degrees.
Grease and flour a 9" round pan.
In a large bowl, combine oil, syrup and egg; stir until well blended. Mix and sift together dry ingredients except for baking soda. Dissolve baking soda in ¾ cup hot water. Add small amounts of hot water/baking soda alternately with portions of the sifted dry ingredients to the oil, syrup and egg mixture until all ingredients are mixed. Pour batter into 9" round prepared pan. Place in preheated 350 degree oven and bake 45 minutes. Remove cake from oven and allow to cool. Before serving, sift powdered sugar onto top of cake.

Upperline

On the dock, lakeside, at Victoria Inn and Gardens

uch of my time goes into my work at *Memphis* magazine and *Memphis Business Quarterly* as Senior Account Executive. My thanks go to my boss, Jeffrey Goldberg, Vice President of Contemporary Media, for his gestures of support as I prepared this book. For hanging in with me throughout the project, thanks go to Joyce and Lester Gingold, my parents.

My thanks go out to all the business owners and staff who provided assistance and information. Thanks go not only to the businesses and business people named in the text, but also to those people not featured, who shared insights and even food---partly out of enthusiasm for Louisiana's culinary heritage and partly out of sheer generosity. David Volion (a.k.a. "Chef Volio"), who owns Volio's Seafood Restaurant in Lafitte and who for many years worked with Paul Prudhomme, comes to mind as a prime example of this enthusiastic and generous type.

My subject matter for this book is New Orleans cuisine, but I must digress: On the wine lists of numerous Crescent City restaurants, I was thrilled to find the delightful and highly regarded organic wines of Lolonis Winery. Back in the mid-1950's, the Lolonis family vineyards went organic and began releasing flights of ladybugs into the vineyards as beneficial predators. Since then, the Lolonis name, organic viticulture and ladybugs have been inextricably linked. Perhaps Lolonis wines and *New Orleans food* should be inextricably linked!

For sharing sterling silver pieces from the late 1800's with me for use in illustrations, thanks go to Karen Wellford of Wellford's Antique Collection in Memphis. Thanks go to Beth Carson, my talented graphic artist, and to Margaret Pellett, my enthusiastic copyeditor, for the time and skill they brought to this publication. We worked as a team to produce *The Art of Dining in New Orleans*.

I have found that New Orleans welcomes people of all ages---a toddler gnawing on French bread in a high chair, a wide-eyed teenager walking down Bourbon Street, a young bride enjoying romance and culture (and shopping like a vulture). For me now, New Orleans is an easy escape from hometown routine.
By air, by Amtrak (take the sleeper!) or even by car, it's not that far! I can get away for a few days and return home feeling pampered and refreshed.

I have loved Nola ever since I can remember. As a long-time fan of this wonderful city, I was deeply saddened by the damage Katrina inflicted. New Orleans natives who have been able to return to their pre-Katrina lives there have dedicated themselves to keeping their rich cultural heritage alive. They are succeeding. Before Katrina, New Orleans was one of the great cities of the world. After Katrina, New Orleans carries on her proud cultural traditions, one of which is world-class cuisine. Naw'lins is still setting the standard in seafood and also offering unique local specialties that amaze and delight, like boudin, andouille, gumbo, jambalaya, muffulettas, and zydeco pies. *Bon appétit!*